Best Climbs
Red Rocks

Best Climbs
Red Rocks

Best Climbs
Red Rocks

JASON D. MARTIN

FALCONGUIDES

GUILFORD, CONNECTICUT

FALCONGUIDES®

An imprint of Rowman & Littlefield
Falcon, FalconGuides, and Outfit Your Mind are registered trademarks of Rowman &
Littlefield.

Distributed by NATIONAL BOOK NETWORK

Photos by author unless otherwise noted.
Maps by Melissa Baker and Alena Pearce © Rowman & Littlefield

British Library Cataloguing-in-Publication Information available
Library of Congress Cataloging in Publication Data available

ISBN 978-1-4930-1963-2 (paperback)
ISBN 978-1-4930-1964-9 (ebook)

The paper used in this publication meets the minimum requirements of American
National Standard for Information Sciences—Permanence of Paper for Printed
Library Materials, ANSI/NISO Z39.48-1992.

WARNING

Climbing is a sport where you may be seriously injured or die. Read this before you use this book.

This guidebook is a compilation of unverified information gathered from many different climbers. The author cannot ensure the accuracy of any of the information in this book, including the topos and route descriptions, the difficulty ratings, and the protection ratings. These may be incorrect or misleading, as ratings of climbing difficulty and danger are always subjective and depend on the physical characteristics (for example, height), experience, technical ability, confidence, and physical fitness of the climber who supplied the rating. Additionally, climbers who achieve first ascents sometimes underrate the difficulty or danger of the climbing route. Therefore, be warned that you must exercise your own judgment on where a climbing route goes, its difficulty, and your ability to safely protect yourself from the risks of rock climbing. Examples of some of these risks are: falling due to technical difficulty or due to natural hazards such as holds breaking, falling rock, climbing equipment dropped by other climbers, hazards of weather and lightning, your own equipment failure, and failure or absence of fixed protection.

You should not depend on any information gleaned from this book for your personal safety; your safety depends on your own good judgment, based on experience and a realistic assessment of your climbing ability. If you have any doubt as to your ability to safely climb a route described in this book, do not attempt it.

The following are some ways to make your use of this book safer:

1. Consultation: You should consult with other climbers about the difficulty and danger of a particular climb prior to attempting it. Most local climbers are glad to give advice on routes in their area; we suggest that you contact locals to confirm ratings and safety of particular routes and to obtain firsthand information about a route chosen from this book.

2. Instruction: The Las Vegas area has a strong community of local climbing instructors and guides available; a list is available in the appendix. We recommend that you engage an instructor or guide to learn safety techniques and to become familiar with the routes and hazards of the areas described in this book. Even after you are proficient in climbing safely, occasional use of a guide is a safe way to raise your climbing standard and learn advanced techniques.

3. Fixed Protection: Some of the routes in this book may use bolts and pitons that are permanently placed in the rock. Because of variances in the manner of placement, weathering, metal fatigue, the quality of the metal used, and many other factors, these fixed protection pieces should always be considered suspect and should always be backed up by equipment that you place yourself. Never depend on a single piece of fixed protection for your safety, because you never can tell whether it will hold weight. In some cases, fixed protection may have been removed or is now missing. However, climbers should not always add new pieces of protection unless existing protection is faulty. Existing protection can be tested by an experienced climber and its strength determined. Climbers are strongly encouraged not to add bolts and drilled pitons to a route. They need to climb the route in the style of the first ascent party (or better) or choose a route within their ability—a route to which they do not have to add additional fixed anchors.

Be aware of the following specific potential hazards that could arise in using this book:

1. Incorrect Descriptions of Routes: If you climb a route and you have a doubt as to where it goes, you should not continue unless you are sure that you can go that way safely. Route descriptions and topos in this book could be inaccurate or misleading.

2. Incorrect Difficulty Rating: A route might be more difficult than the rating indicates. Do not be lulled into a false sense of security by the difficulty rating.

3. Incorrect Protection Rating: If you climb a route and you are unable to arrange adequate protection from the risk of falling through the use of fixed pitons or bolts and by placing your own protection devices, do not assume that there is adequate protection available higher just because the route protection rating indicates the route does not have an X or an R rating. Every route is potentially an X (a fall may be deadly), due to the inherent hazards of climbing—including, for example, failure or absence of fixed protection, your own equipment's failure, or improper use of climbing equipment.

There are no warranties, whether expressed or implied, that this guidebook is accurate or that the information contained in it is reliable. There are no warranties of fitness for a particular purpose or that this guide is merchantable. Your use of this book indicates your assumption of the risk that it may contain errors and is an acknowledgment of your own sole responsibility for your climbing safety.

Contents

Overview

N

Kilometers
Miles

1. Highway 215
2. The Strip
3. Red Rock Campground
4. Calico Basin
5. Red Rock Scenic Drive
6. Black Velvet/Windy Peak Area
7. West Charleston Blvd/Highway 159

Dedication

This book is for my son, Caden Jase.
"The power of the imagination makes us infinite."

—John Muir

Like father like son

Acknowledgments

This book would not have been possible without the generous time, help, and support from a number of people. These include Fran Baker, Larry DeAngelo, Jared Drapala, Wyatt Evanson, Krista Eytchison, Dunham Gooding, Blake Herrington, Michael Kimm, Tom Kirby, Michael Layton, Christopher Marshall, Zach Novak, James Pierson, Alasdair Turner, John Wilder, and Dan Young.

In addition to the preceding, I would like to thank Natasha and Dave Costello. Natasha, an old friend and coworker, recommended me for this project. And Dave—Natasha's husband—played the indispensable role of editor for this book. Dave is not only an editor, but is also an author. Check out his epic adventure narrative, *Flying Off Everest: A Journey from the Summit to the Sea*.

There were three individuals who did a great deal more than all the rest put together. American Alpine Institute guides Doug Foust, Andy Stephen, and Andrew Yasso are three of the best mountain guides you could find, anywhere. I am deeply indebted to them for all their help with this book. They provided excellent critiques of the beta, thoughts on content, and excellent photos. If you're looking for a guide in Red Rock Canyon, you can't do much better than any one of these three.

And finally, I'd like to thank all those who have written about Red Rock Canyon in the past, be it in guidebooks, in articles, or online. Climbing is a complex art, and understanding mountain features is difficult. The continuing flow of information in each of these forms adds to our collective knowledge of the Red Rocks of Southern Nevada.

Introduction

Las Vegas.

This is a place known throughout the world as Sin City. It's a place where people come to lose themselves in their fantasies. It's a place where people come to reinvent themselves. Some come to pretend they're someone they're not: a high roller, a millionaire, a player, or a celebrity. Others come to relish in who they actually are: a foodie, an audience member, a gambler, or maybe even a climber.

With over 41 million visitors every year, Las Vegas continues to be one of the hottest vacation destinations on the planet. Visitors come for the glitz. They come for the glamour. They come for the gaming. They come for the shows. They come for the food. They come for the shopping. They come for the nightlife.

And they come for the climbing!

The Red Rock Canyon National Conservation Area—a place affectionately known as Red Rocks by climbers the world over—sports thousands of boulder problems, sport routes, and traditional climbs. It is considered one of the biggest climbing tourist destinations in North America. Indeed, the Bureau of Land Management (BLM) estimates that the conservation area supports up to 80,000 climber user days every year.

So why are all these climbers visiting Red Rock Canyon?

There are two reasons.

First, Las Vegas was built for tourists. The place is easy to access. Flights to the city are cheap. Rental cars are reasonable. Hotel rooms are abundant, and there's a lot to do on rest days.

And second, the climbing is stellar. One day you can crank up a wildly overhanging sport route, and on the next you can cruise up a six-pitch moderate. Some people choose to do both on the same day! The variety in Red Rock is absolutely unparalleled.

Las Vegas is a place where people come to lose themselves in their fantasies, and climbers are no different. Most visitors try to fulfill those fantasies in the adult Disneyland that is Sin City. But a few of us know the truth. Dreams don't come true on the Strip. They come true in the desert, on the cliffs, crags, and mountains of the Red Rocks of Southern Nevada.

How to Get to Red Rock Canyon National Conservation Area

Red Rock Canyon National Conservation Area is approximately 20 miles west of the world-famous Las Vegas Strip. The jagged peaks and deep valleys of the conservation area can easily be seen from many locations on the Strip. There are three possible driving routes to Red Rock.

North Strip and Downtown Approach

If staying on the northern end of the Strip, staying in downtown, or entering the city from the north, the best approach to Red Rock is via Charleston Boulevard (NV 159). Find Charleston Boulevard approximately halfway between the Stratosphere Hotel and Casino and the Downtown Arts District. Charleston intersects both Las Vegas Boulevard and I-15. To reach Red Rock Canyon, take Charleston west toward the mountains for approximately 30 minutes. Just past the Red Rock Hotel and Casino, cross I-215 and drive 6 miles to the entrance gate to the Red Rock Canyon Scenic Drive.

South Strip Approach

If you choose to stay south of Sahara Boulevard, if you're starting from the airport, or if you are approaching the city from the south on I-15, the best way to access Red Rock is via I-215, which intersects both Las Vegas Boulevard and I-15 approximately 1.7 miles south of Mandalay Bay Hotel and Casino. From the south end of Las Vegas Boulevard, drive I-215 west for approximately 14 miles. Exit onto Charleston Boulevard and turn left (west). Follow Charleston for approximately 6 miles to the entrance to the Red Rock Canyon Scenic Drive.

NV 160 Approach

NV 160 bisects Las Vegas Boulevard and I-15 a few miles south of I-215 near the Silverton Hotel and Casino. This approach is recommended for those who are staying near the Silverton or anywhere south of the main Las Vegas Strip. NV 160 meets NV 159 at a T intersection approximately 11 miles west of Las Vegas Boulevard. From NV 160 turn right onto NV 159 and drive 10.4 miles to the entrance to the Red Rock Canyon Scenic Drive.

Camping

The BLM operates a fee campground just outside Red Rock Canyon Scenic Drive, approximately 2 miles east of the conservation area entrance. Group sites (ten people or more) are available for reservation. To book a group site, log onto recreation.gov.

During the peak spring season, campsites can be difficult to find. Climbers should work together, share sites, and try to accommodate all members of the tribe. However, if there are no sites available, free primitive camping is available in Lovell Canyon, approximately 30 minutes from the entrance to the scenic drive.

To access Lovell Canyon from the Red Rock Campground, continue west on NV 159. Turn right (west) onto NV 160 and drive approximately 10 minutes to the pass and Mountain Springs. Lovell Canyon Road is approximately 5 miles beyond Mountain Springs on the left. Drive along the road until you find a suitable primitive campsite. No camping gear should be left unattended while away from your site in this area.

No matter where you camp, expect wind. Reinforce your tent tie-downs. Some climbers collapse their tents at the campground and place rocks on top of the collapsed structures while they are away when high winds are predicted.

Several hotels and casinos have RV parks. The pricing for these varies dramatically from one location to the next. Popular RV parks include Circus Circus, Sam's Town, and the Las Vegas RV Resort.

Many climbers have experimented with bivying in casino parking lots. Occasionally this works out, and occasionally it doesn't . . .

Hotels and Motels

Las Vegas is a world-class tourist destination with over 100,000 hotel rooms. With that in mind, it may seem odd that there are weekends when it is hard to find a room. Be sure to book early.

There are several websites that allow you to shop for cheap hotel rooms on a last-minute basis. Among many others these include hotwire.com, kayak.com, priceline.com, and hotels.com. If you get lucky, you might find a last-minute deal on one of these sites for less than $75 a night.

If you're price sensitive, but don't want to wait for a last-minute deal, you can often find economical rooms with flimsy walls in downtown Las Vegas near the Fremont Street Experience. Hotels here include the Golden Nugget, the Plaza, the 4 Queens, the D Las Vegas, the California, the El Cortez, and the Downtown Grand Casino and Hotel. Some of these rooms go for as little as $25 a night—but you get what you pay for.

If you have the means, then you should choose a quality hotel that provides easy access to the conservation area. Following is a list of some climber favorites.

Old Nevada, Bonnie Springs (bonniesprings.com)

The motel at Bonnie Springs is a mere 10-minute drive from the Red Rock Canyon Scenic Drive. This is a rural motel in the desert on NV 159. They have a small restaurant, but little else. This is the perfect place if you want to get away from the bustle of Las Vegas.

Red Rock Casino Resort and Spa (redrock.sclv.com)

This "higher-end" hotel and casino is approximately a 10-minute drive from the Red Rock Canyon Scenic Drive. It has numerous restaurants, spas, stores, a bowling alley, and movie theaters inside. It is also across the street from the popular climber brewpub hangout, BJ's Brewery.

The Suncoast (suncoastcasino.com)

This is an economical alternative to the Red Rock Casino. The Suncoast is about 20 minutes from the scenic drive, on Rampart, almost directly across the street from an REI store. This is a hotel and casino with several restaurants, a movie theater, and a bowling alley.

The Strip

If you wish to stay on the Strip, the hotels on the southern end provide the easiest access to I-215, the highway used to access Red Rocks. Hotels on the south end of the Strip include, but are not limited to, Excalibur, Luxor, Mandalay Bay, and Tropicana. These hotels are approximately 35 minutes from the scenic drive.

How to Use This Book

Red Rock Canyon National Conservation Area is the adventure climbing capital of the country. Many of the climbs are moderate, but they can be long and complex. You'll find route topos and descriptions here, but remember, these are just suggestions. If there are other parties on a route and things are crowded, consider climbing a variation or building an anchor in a place other than the -suggested spot. Be creative out there and have fun!

Ratings

This book uses a combination of the Yosemite Decimal System (YDS) and the commitment grade system. As a rock climber you are probably already well aware of the YDS rating scale. Some may not be as familiar with the commitment grade system. This is a system that estimates a route's length and complexity for a competent party that is climbing at or above the YDS grade listed for a given route. Commonly the approach and descent is left out of commitment grades. However, in this book, the commitment grade includes both of these, as there are some extremely technical approaches and descents.

Commitment grades will vary based on the climber. A party that is climbing at their limit may find a Grade III route to be a 12-hour endeavor, while a strong, experienced party might dispatch the same route in a couple of hours.

The commitment grade system is as follows:

Grade I—A route that takes an hour or less to complete. The sport climbs and single-pitch lines in this book are all Grade I routes.

Grade II—A route that takes a few hours to complete. These are often approximately three to five technical pitches in length. The approach and descent are generally straightforward.

Grade III—A route that takes 5 to 8 hours for a competent party to complete. These lines often have approximately five to seven pitches of technical

climbing. There may be some difficulty with the approach, and the descent may be less straightforward.

Grade IV—A route that takes 8 to 12 hours for a competent party to complete, with approximately eight to fifteen technical pitches. The approach and/or the descent may be complex or difficult.

Grade V—A route that takes a competent party in excess of 12 hours to complete, usually with sixteen or more pitches. Many parties require a bivy on such a long route. The approach and descent may require several hours to negotiate. Getting lost is a real possibility.

In addition to the grade system, some routes may be marked with an R or an X. An R rating on a route indicates that there are some runouts where a fall could result in serious injury. An X rating indicates that a fall could result in death. Climbers should feel confident in their climbing movement skills before attempting a route with an R or an X rating.

Protection and Gear

Most multi-pitch climbers in Red Rock carry a rack of wires, two or three micro-cams, and a full set of cams up to 3 inches. The standard Red Rock rack includes double cams from approximately 0.5 inch to 2 inches. Most multi-pitch routes require gear up to 4 inches.

If you are climbing at your limit or there are long pitches, you may desire doubles in larger gear. Some climbers carry triples of certain sizes on long, challenging pitches.

In this guidebook it's assumed that the preceding is a standard rack for the area. Most descriptions will tell you what the largest gear is that you might need for a pitch.

Ethics

While visiting the Red Rock Canyon National Conservation Area, Leave No Trace (LNT) principles should be employed at all times. The basic concepts of LNT are as follows:

- Plan Ahead and Prepare
- Travel and Camp on Durable Surfaces
- Dispose of Waste Properly
- Leave What You Find
- Minimize Campfire Impacts
- Respect Wildlife
- Be Considerate of Other Visitors

Following is a breakdown of these principles and how they should be employed in Red Rock Canyon National Conservation Area.

Plan Ahead and Prepare

In the desert environment it is important to have the right clothing for the season, as well as food, water, and sunscreen. Know where you are going and follow established trails. If it is at all possible that you will be inside the conservation area after it closes, call for a late exit permit (702-515-5050).

Routes in the canyon can be long and arduous. Be sure to bring a cell phone and appropriate phone numbers. If caught out overnight, be sure that no one initiates a rescue unless one is really needed.

It's not a bad idea to bring extra webbing or cordage to help facilitate descents or retreat. Be sure to check all previously installed rappel materials. With 300 days of sun every year, UV damage can happen quickly. If you suspect a problem, beef up the anchor.

Travel and Camp on Durable Surfaces

The desert environment is fragile. Follow established trails and avoid cutting across the desert where there are no trails.

Backcountry camping is not permitted in Red Rock Canyon unless on one of the longer lines in the conservation area. For more information on routes and walls where it is possible to bivy, call the Red Rock Late Exit Line at (702) 515-5050.

Dispose of Waste Properly

Anything packed in should also be packed out. In other words, litter—including cigarette butts and toilet paper—should be disposed of properly.

Human waste is a tremendous problem in Red Rock Canyon. Many people place small rocks on top of big piles of toilet paper and feces, or just smear it all over belay stations. This is not a good way to deal with your poo.

Perhaps the best way to deal with said human waste is to pack it out. You can use two plastic bags or a commercial waste bag like a WAG Bag, a Biffy Bag, or a Rest Stop.

In 2012 American Alpine Institute guide and Southern Nevada Climbers Coalition board member Scott Massey installed waste bag dispensers on the trail to Black Velvet Canyon, the Mescalito, near the entrance to the Black Corridor, on the approach to The Gallery and the Panty Wall area, and on the trail to the Kraft Boulders. These boxes dispense commercial waste bags that are meant for human fecal matter.

A waste bag dispenser in Calico Basin

Climbers

Do your part to keep Red Rock clean.
Take a waste bag with you. Use as directed.

DISPOSE IN ANY TRASH CONTAINER

DO NOT PUT IN ANY TOILET OR LEAVE IN THE FIELD

Take It!   Use It!   Pack It!   Lose It!

Please donate $3 to cover the cost of each bag.
Donation boxes are available at Desert Rock Sports and Red Rock
Climbing Center.

This service is courtesy of the Las Vegas Climbers Liaison
Council, and is funded by the American Alpine Club's
Cornerstone Conservation Grant, the Access Fund, and
Mountain Gear.

The first option should always be to use a waste bag, but if it is not possible to do this, then you should cat hole your waste. In other words, choose a location that is at least 200 feet from any creek beds, trails, or the base of climbing areas and dig a 6-inch-deep hole. Bury your waste in the hole and pack out the toilet paper.

If you find yourself on a route without a waste bag, do not smear fecal matter all over the rock next to your belay station or on the route. Instead, try to get away from any place where people will be climbing or belaying before using the bathroom. If there is no place to bury the waste, then smear it thinly on the wall away from the route, any adjacent route, or any belay stations. The waste should be smeared so thinly that rain and sun will quickly break it down. Pack out all toilet paper. But remember, this is an emergency technique and is not the preferred alternative. It would be better to simply carry a waste bag or a couple of ziplocks to carry everything out.

Urine can also be a problem. Try not to urinate on handholds; the next climber will be much more appreciative if they don't have to put their hands in your pee. Urinate away from the base of the route if possible. Try to do so on rocks in the sun. This will help break down the urine and eliminate the smell.

Leave What You Find
Native American arrowheads, lush cacti, animal bones, and blooming flowers abound in Red Rock Canyon. When you come upon any of these items, they should be recognized for their beauty in their environment. These things lose their value when they are removed from where they are found.

Minimize Campfire Impacts
Campfires are not permitted within the Red Rock Canyon National Conservation Area. Be sure that all fires in established fire pits within the campground are completely out before leaving them unattended.

There have been a number of wildfires both inside and outside the scenic drive over the last several years. Ignorant people flicking cigarette butts out of car windows started many of these fires. Please do not do this.

Respect Wildlife
The wild burros are wild burros for a reason. The animals can be dangerous. People have been both bitten and kicked by burros. Taking pictures of these animals and enjoying their beauty from a distance is a fine endeavor. But there is no reason to feed these animals or try to pet them. This encourages them to congregate on the road, where they are likely to be hit by a car, potentially injuring both the animal and the driver.

Tarantulas, rattlesnakes, and chuckwallas should be left alone. Likewise, desert tortoises and gila monsters should not be disturbed in any way. These animals are delicate, and any human interaction may seriously harm them. There is no reason to mess with any of the local wildlife.

Be Considerate of Other Visitors

Be aware of your impact on other visitors. If you are loud or rude, you're playing loud music, or you have an obnoxious dog, be aware that this may have a negative impact on someone else's experience.

While toproping or sport climbing, be sure to share routes with other parties. It is not acceptable to leave ropes hanging all over a wall so that a few people can climb while barring others from doing the same. Be courteous.

A burro skull found near Black Velvet Canyon. The treasure wasn't the physical skull, but the act of finding it. This was an incredibly cool discovery that I will always remember. We left the skull with the rest of the skeleton for the next party to find, and to hopefully have a similar experience.

Many of the multi-pitch routes in this book are very popular climbs. Passing slow parties and getting passed by faster parties are normal occurrences. But there are a few ground rules to passing:

- Before trying to pass, be sure that you actually are faster than the party you're trying to pass. Conversely, if you are being passed, make sure the passing party is faster than you. It doesn't make sense for parties that are moving at the same pace to pass one another. Indeed, it often causes a traffic jam, slowing down everyone on the route.
- Be polite to other parties on the rock. Ask before passing. If someone asks and they appear to be faster than you, grant them permission to pass. If you ask and the slower party says no, continue to be courteous. Ultimately, they got there before you and have the right to be on the route ahead of you. Do not pass them anyway.
- Passing should be done in a safe manner. Use a variation or pass at a ledge. Don't lead up underneath someone who is already leading—this is a recipe for disaster.

Rainy Days

The Aztec sandstone found in Red Rock Canyon is fragile. It is particularly fragile during and after a rainstorm. It is considered poor form to climb on wet rock, as a broken hold may change the nature of a climb forever.

If the ground is damp near your climb, then the stone is likely saturated and holds may break. If the ground is dry and the sand is powdery, then it is likely that your route is sufficiently dry for climbing.

BLM Rules and Regulations

The Bureau of Land Management manages Red Rock Canyon National Conservation Area. BLM rangers patrol the scenic drive, Calico Basin, and the desert south of the scenic drive. To avoid a ticket, follow all posted speed limits, don't feed the burros, don't touch the tortoises, and obtain late exit permits when you expect to be late.

To obtain a late exit permit, call (702) 515-5050. When the answering machine picks up, be ready with the following information:

Name, address, and phone number
Vehicle license and vehicle description
Type of pass (late exit or overnight)
Parking area
Route name
Date of climb

Scenic Drive Hours

November–February	6 a.m.–5 p.m.
March	6 a.m.–7 p.m.
April–September	6 a.m.–8 p.m.
October	6 a.m.–7 p.m.

Scenic Drive and Red Rock Canyon Fee Schedule
Private vehicle—$7
Motorcycle—$3
Bicycle—$3
Pedestrian—$3
Annual Pass—$30
America the Beautiful National Parks and Federal Recreation Pass—$80

Bolting

Bolting is currently permitted in the non-wilderness areas of the Calico Hills. In other words, new bolts may still be placed in most of Calico Basin (the wilderness line is in Gateway Canyon behind Kraft Mountain), the First and the Second Pullout, as well as in most of Sandstone Quarry. The line is a bit fuzzy in Sandstone. If you can see the parking lot, you're probably okay, but if not, you should double-check.

Beautiful bighorn sheep in Red Rock Canyon
PHOTO BY ALASDAIR TURNER

As of this writing, new bolts are not permitted in the canyons west of the Calico Hills. However, you may obtain a permit to replace old bolts with a hand drill.

For more information on current bolting rules and restrictions and to find out exactly where the wilderness lines are, contact the BLM Las Vegas Field Office at (702) 515-5000.

Season

Though people climb in Red Rock throughout the year, the area tends to be a fall, winter, and spring destination. The climbing season starts in late September and ends in late May. The most popular months for climbers to visit are October, November, March, and April. Climbers often overlook the mild temperatures during the winter months of December, January, and February, and the area tends to be less crowded in those time frames. Boulderers, however, have discovered the cool months, and weekends are busy throughout the winter.

Even though Red Rock Canyon is a desert environment and summer temperatures soar well above 100°F, visiting climbers should be prepared for all possible weather. Rain, snow, and high winds occur in Red Rock throughout the climbing season. On the other hand, climbers may encounter 70-degree temperatures in the dead of winter. Climbers should be prepared for both extremes.

Temperatures and Rainfall

Month	Average High (degrees)	Average Low (degrees)	Average Rainfall (inches)
January	54	29	1.5
February	57	32	1.8
March	64	38	2
April	71	45	0.5
May	81	53	0.2
June	91	63	0.1
July	96	71	0.8
August	94	68	1
September	88	59	0.5
October	75	47	0.3
November	62	36	0.7
December	53	29	0.7

Climb Finder
Best Crags for Toproping
Moderate Mecca
Cannibal Crag
Cowlick Crag
Cut Your Teeth Crag
The Hamlet
Amusement Park

Top 10 Best Trad Single-Pitch Routes
Tonto (5.5.), Ragged Edges Area
Doobie Dance (5.6), Romper Room
Fender Bender (5.6), Front Slab
Romper Room (5.7), Romper Room
Ragged Edges (5.8), Ragged Edges Area
Valentines Day (5.8+), Moderate Mecca
Black Track (5.9), Hidden Falls Wall
Panty Line (5.10a), Panty Wall
Left Out (5.10d), Hidden Falls Wall
The Fox (5.10d), The Fox Wall

Top 10 Best Multi-pitch Routes
Cat in the Hat (5.6+, II+), Pine Creek Canyon
Olive Oil (5.7, III), Juniper Canyon
Birdland (5.7+, II+), Pine Creek Canyon
Frogland (5.8, III), Black Velvet Canyon
Crimson Chrysalis (5.8+, IV), Juniper Canyon
Epinephrine (5.9, IV+), Black Velvet Canyon
Black Orpheus (5.10a, IV), Oak Creek Canyon
Triassic Sands (5.10b, III), Black Velvet Canyon
Levitation 29 (5.11c, IV+), Oak Creek Canyon
Cloud Tower (5.11d, IV), Juniper Canyon

Top 10 Best Sport Climbs
Frailty, Thy Name Is Sandstone (5.7), The Hamlet
Man's Best Friend (5.7), Winston Wall
Big Bad Wolf (5.9), Riding Hood Wall
Vagabonds (5.10a), Black Corridor
Byzantium (5.10b), Civilization Crags
Roto-Hammer (5.10c), Stone Wall
Rebel Without a Pause (5.11a), Black Corridor
Caustic (5.11b), Cannibal Crag
Yaak Crack (5.11c), The Gallery

Best Adventure Climbs
Prime Rib (5.7, II)
Algae on Parade (5.7+, II+)
Sunspot Ridge (5.8, IV)
Dark Shadows (To the Top! 5.9, IV)
Resolution Arête (5.10d C1 or 5.11d, V)

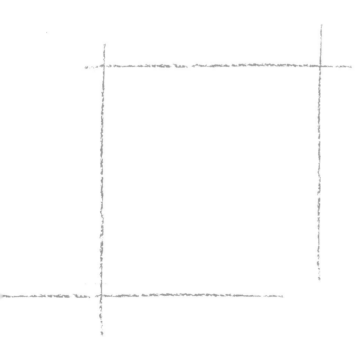

Map Legend

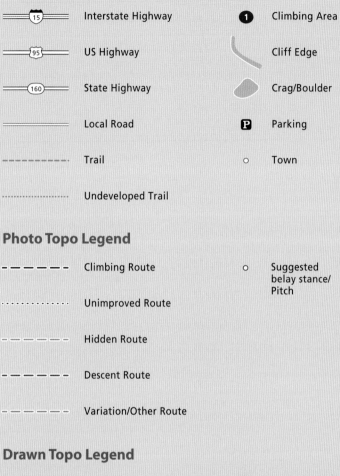

Interstate Highway	Climbing Area
US Highway	Cliff Edge
State Highway	Crag/Boulder
Local Road	Parking
Trail	Town
Undeveloped Trail	

Photo Topo Legend

Climbing Route	Suggested belay stance/ Pitch
Unimproved Route	
Hidden Route	
Descent Route	
Variation/Other Route	

Drawn Topo Legend

Ledge	Pitch Number
Roof	Bolt
Left-Facing Corner	Tree
Right-Facing Corner	Face Climbing
Arête	Crack
Groove	

1.

Calico Basin

Calico Basin comprises several crags on the northeast side of the Calico Hills. The climbing area is snuggled up to the cliffbands above a handful of rural private plots of land.

The area harbors dozens of single-pitch climbs and a few multi-pitch lines as well. One of the main attractions to the Calico Basin is the fact that, at the time of this writing, parking was free, and you do not have to enter the Red Rock Canyon Scenic Drive to access the climbing here.

Climbers should be respectful of private property in the basin. This area has been a flashpoint with local property owners due to parking problems, loud profanity, loud music, and marijuana use. To ensure continued access, climbers should follow the parking rules, turn the music down, avoid loud profanity, and avoid the use of illicit drugs in the parking areas or on Sandstone Drive near people's homes.

Approach

The road to Calico Basin is just a short distance west of the campground. Take the first right-hand turn past Moenkopi Road. Drive a short distance through the semi-residential area to the Red Springs parking lot.

As stated previously, Calico Basin is not inside the Red Rock Canyon Scenic Drive. However, the Red Springs parking area follows the same time schedule as the rest of the conservation area.

If there is a possibility that you will not return to your car until after closing time, either park at the "Elbow" or at the bouldering parking area at the end of Sandstone Drive.

To get to the Elbow, continue past the entrance to Red Springs and turn right onto Calico Drive; continue for 100 yards and then turn left onto Assisi Canyon Drive. Continue for another hundred yards and park nose in at the fence where the road makes a sharp turn right onto Sandstone Drive.

To park at the end of Sandstone Drive, continue past the Elbow to the end of the road approximately half a mile down. Turn left onto the old road that has been turned into a parking area and park.

Please note that several new No Parking signs have been installed on the roads in this area. Additionally, Calico Basin parking areas are generally for dawn-to-dusk parking only. Cars left overnight may be ticketed.

Calico Basin

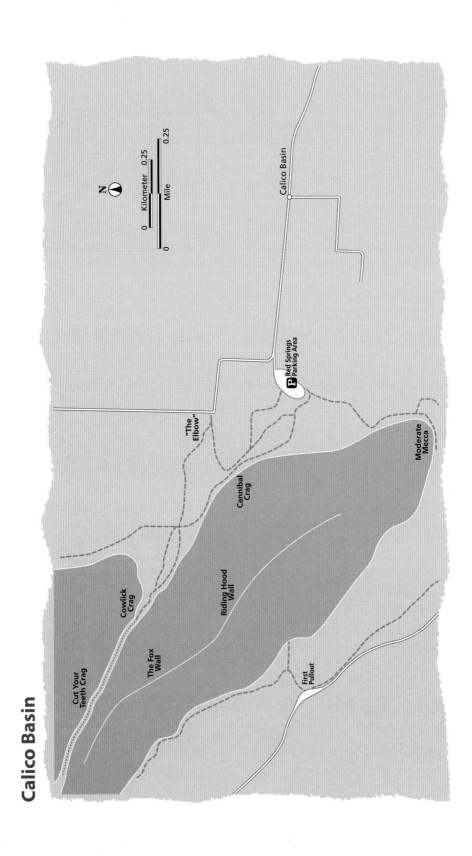

MODERATE MECCA

In the early 2000s the top of Moderate Mecca was commonly used for hippie drum circles. But then the Red Springs Picnic Area was renovated, the boardwalk was added, and hordes of families and tourists began to arrive in the area. Many started to make the short climb up the hill to the top of the crag. And then, suddenly, the hippies were gone, replaced by tourists who couldn't help but stand on the cliff's edge to take selfies, making the climbers below unbearably nervous.

Alas, the tourists still climb to the top of the crag to look down, and though it can be a bit disconcerting, Moderate Mecca continues to be extremely popular with climbers. The area is sunny year-round and harbors a large number of easy to moderate climbs as well as numerous toprope options. There are also a lot of lizards there!

Approach: To access Moderate Mecca, drive to Calico Basin and park in the Red Springs parking area. At the end of the lot, just to the left of the wooden walkway, is a trail that cuts up and to the south outside the wooden fence. Follow this trail up to the crest. Drop down the trail and take the first possible right to access the base of the main crag. To access the bottom of Side Effects, continue down the trail and take the second possible right. **Time:** 15 minutes.

Sun Exposure: Moderate Mecca is exposed to the sun all day.

Types of Climbing Available:
Trad, sport, mixed, toprope

1. Side Effects (5.10b, 80 feet, sport, TR) A super-fun sport climb that requires a number of interesting body positions. This route climbs up the giant tower that sits just below the main Moderate Mecca area. 5 bolts. **FA:** Mike Ward, 1991.

2. Stew on This (5.10a, 40 feet, mixed, TR) The bottom of this route is easily found, as it starts at a small roof with a bolt directly above it. Crank through the first steep move and then plug a cam (#2–2.5) into the crack. Clip the second bolt and be careful on the flake that one online commenter wrote, "groans like my grandma listening to rap music." Pro to 3 inches. **FA:** Kevin Campbell and Todd Swain, 1998.

3. Is It Soup Yet (5.10b, 40 feet, mixed, TR) Found just left of Stew on This. Power through the little roof at the first bolt, then climb the crack to the anchor for Stew on This. Small gear (wires or a small cam) make this route a reasonable ascent. **FA:** Kevin Campbell and Todd Swain, 1998.

4. Chicken Soup for the Soul (aka Soup Nazi) (5.10a, 40 feet, TR) Climb up the steep face between Is It Soup Yet and Chicken Gumbo for Your Dumbo. This route is primarily a toprope, but it has been led

Moderate Mecca

To Moderate Mecca

on extremely thin gear. If you elect to lead it, this route is rated X. **FA:** Teresa Krolak, Patty Gill, and Todd Swain, 1999.

5. Chicken Gumbo for Your Dumbo (5.6, 40 feet, trad, TR) Climb up the easy corner system to the left of Chicken Soup for the Soul. This route and Chicken Soup share the same start. Climb through a small roof that's easier than it looks to attain the left-facing corner. Pro to 3 inches. **FA:** Todd Swain, Patty Gill, and Teresa Krolak, 1999.

6. Soupy Sales (5.6, 35 feet, trad, TR) Immediately left of Chicken Gumbo is a second corner system with a crack running up it. Soupy Sales is fun, but

there is a bit of choss on it. Pro to 3 inches. **FA:** Todd Swain, Patty Gill, and Teresa Krolak, 1999.

7. From Soup to Nuts (5.7, 40 feet, trad, TR) This climb is the crack left of the corner system. An awkward start leads to easier climbing. Large gear may be useful. Pro to 4 inches. **FA:** Todd Swain, Patty Gill, and Teresa Krolak, 1999.

8. The Singing Love Pen (5.9, 40 feet, trad, TR) Found approximately 30 feet left of From Soup to Nuts, this line follows a crack up a right-facing corner through a bulge. Pro to 4 inches. **FA:** Todd Swain, Patty Gill, and Teresa Krolak, 1999.

Moderate Mecca

9. Valentines Day (5.8+, 50 feet, trad, TR) The best route at the crag! Valentines Day sends the next corner system to the left of The Singing Love Pen. Jam and lieback up the perfect hand crack in the left-facing corner to a bolted anchor. Pro to 3 inches. **FA:** Randal Grandstaff and Danny Ridder, 1988.

10. Ace of Hearts (5.10d, 50 feet, TR) This line shares an anchor with Valentines Day and is found immediately left of it. Crank up thin crimps and cracks to the anchor. This route has been led on sketchy gear.
FA: Unknown.

11. Immoral (5.10b, 80 feet, sport, TR) Approximately 15 feet left of Ace of Hearts is a smooth face with a small roof at the base. Immoral climbs the right-hand bolt line up to a traverse, then joins Immoderate at the top. 4 bolts. **FA:** Pier Marsh and Randy Marsh.

12. Immoderate (5.9, A0, 80 feet, sport, TR) Just left of Immoral is a roof with a bolt above it. Stick clip the bolt and then crank on the draw. Continue up to the shared anchor. **FA:** Pier Marsh and Randy Marsh.

13. Abbey Road (5.4, 140 feet, trad) Abbey Road is the crazy fun face and corner system found approximately 5 minutes left of Immoderate. Start at the small tower. **Pitch 1:** Climb up to a corner, then launch out left following a thin crack to a small roof and up to the midpoint anchors (5.4, 90 feet). **Pitch 2:** Continue up less-appealing rock to the top of the formation (5.0, 100 feet). **Descent:** From the top, walk off to the right. From the top of pitch 1, rappel to the base. Pro to 3 inches. **FA:** Unknown.

14. Fleet Street (5.8 R, 50 feet, sport) Climb up the thin face, passing two bolts to the left of Abbey Road. To toprope this climb, send Abbey Road and set up toprope anchors at the top of the first pitch. Pro to 2 inches. **FA:** Kevin Campbell and Todd Swain, 1998.

15. Muckraker (5.8, 85 feet, trad) Climb up the corner left of Fleet Street. The first few moves through the small roof provide for an interesting and cruxy start. A large cam may be useful. **FA:** Todd Swain and Paul Ross, 1998.

16. Scalawag (5.10b, 90 feet, trad) Power through the wild roof left of Muckraker. Most people can protect the lower climbing with a #2 and a #3 size cam, but some may wish to have something bigger. A green Big Bro is helpful. Blast up to the sling material wrapped around the pillar, which is the fixed anchor for the route. Be sure to check the webbing before rappelling. Pro to 4 inches. **FA:** Todd Swain and Paul Ross, 1988.

Not all the climbers at Moderate Mecca are human. This is also a spectacular place for "lizard viewing."
PHOTO BY ALASDAIR TURNER

CANNIBAL CRAG

This giant boulder perched on the hill above the Elbow parking area is home to some phenomenal sport climbs. The short approach and the friendly routes have made this crag super popular with locals and visitors alike. As it is easy to walk to the top of this crag, many routes may be toproped. Those routes that are easily toproped are identified in the following descriptions. However, nearly every route on the crag can be toproped with a little bit of ingenuity.

Of particular note is the Caustic (5.11b) route, one of the most photogenic routes in the entire conservation area. It's also on our list of best sport climbs. Indeed, many consider it to be one of the best in the area. It is absolutely well worth the burn.

Approach: Park at the Red Springs Picnic Area. From the lot take one of the trails that head northwest—in other words, any trail right of the boardwalk. Follow the trail toward the large freestanding boulder. **Time:** 10 minutes. Alternatively, you can park at the Elbow and scramble directly up to Cannibal Crag. **Time:** 5 minutes.

Sun Exposure: The sun shifts around Cannibal Crag throughout the day, and at least one aspect is always sunny. The whole crag falls into the shade in the late afternoon.

Types of Climbing Available: Trad, sport, mixed, toprope, face and crack climbing

The lines on Cannibal Crag are listed from left to right, starting at the seriously overhung face on the left side of the south face.

1. A Modest Proposal (5.5, 30 feet, TR) Buried deep behind the Cannibal Crag boulder is a ramp that may be used to get to the top. This little toprope problem sends the face up to a seam right of the access ramp. From the top of the crag, the line is quite obvious as it comes up the crack to a small green shrub located below a bolt. It takes some creative anchoring to set up the toprope. **FA:** Unknown.

2. Man-Eater (5.12a, 30 feet, sport) Found just to the right of A Modest Proposal. Climb up steep terrain, passing four bolts to an anchor. This line has eaten more than a few women too . . . 4 bolts. **FA:** Dan McQuade, 1992.

3. Wonderstuff (5.12d, 30 feet, sport) The second bolted line on the south face starts about 8 feet right of Man-Eater. The first bolt is high, and a stick clip is recommended. 4 bolts. **FA:** Paul Van Betten, Richard Harrison, and Sal Mamusia, 1991.

4. New Wave Hookers (5.12c, 35 feet, sport) Found right of Wonderstuff. Climb up honeycombed rock to mussy hook anchors. There is groundfall potential, and you should consider stick clipping the second bolt. 5 bolts.

Cannibal Crag

FA: Paul Van Betten, Richard Harrison, Sal Mamusia, 1991.

5. Fear this Sport (5.12b, 30 feet, sport) This is the last of the steep sport lines on the south face. Look for it 10 feet right of New Wave Hookers. This is a very bouldery line for very bouldery people. 5 bolts. **FA:** Paul Van Betten, Richard Harrison, and Sal Mamusia, 1991.

6. Caliban (5.8+ R, 80 feet, mixed, TR) The most obvious feature on the east face of the Cannibal Crag is the left-leaning crack climb called You Are What You Eat. Caliban is found approximately 20 feet left and uphill of the base of that crack. There are only three bolts on this precarious route. You may

be able to supplement the bolts with a .5 or .75 cam. However, Caliban is much more fun (and less stressful) as a toprope. 3 bolts. **FA:** Paul Van Betten and Sal Mamusia, 1993.

7. You Are What You Eat (5.5 or 5.9, 85 feet, trad, TR) This is the obvious crack that splits the east face. There are two potential starts: The left-hand start will keep the line an easy 5.5, whereas the right-hand start will bump up the first moves to 5.9. This line shares anchors with Caliban. Pro to 3 inches. **FA:** Unknown.

8. Suck Up My Baseboy (5.10d, 60 feet, mixed) Climb up the right-hand crack at the start of You Are What You Eat and then continue out onto the face. A line of four bolts will appear, leading to the right and up to the anchor. **FA:** Paul Van Betten, Richard Harrison, and Sal Mamusia, 1991.

9. Baseboy Direct (5.11b, 60 feet, sport) This is a variation of Suck Up My Baseboy that avoids the use of the crack. Climb up past seven bolts to the mussy hook anchor. 7 bolts. **FA:** Pier and Randy Marsh, 1997.

10. Save the Heart and Eat It Later (5.12a, 60 feet, sport) Found just right of Baseboy Direct and immediately left of some faded graffiti, this line sends the middle of the face. A technical route, the holds get smaller the higher you go, and seem to disappear at the fourth bolt. 5 bolts. **FA:** Paul Van Betten, Richard Harrison, Sal Mamusia, and Shelby Shelton, 1991.

11. Pickled (5.11c, 50 feet, sport) Start as for Save the Heart and Eat It Later, but cut right after the first bolt. Continue up and right past four bolts to a mussy hook anchor. 5 bolts. **FA:** Paul Van Betten, Richard Harrison, and Sal Mamusia, 1991.

12. Caustic (5.11b, 50 feet, sport) The most photogenic route in the area! Climb the beautiful exposed arête to a mussy hook anchor. For some the crux of the route is trying to pose for the camera while hiding the fact that their harness is clipped directly to a bolt hidden by their body. And for

others the crux is making the fourth clip. 4 bolts. **FA:** Dan Kruleski, Shelby Shelton, Paul Van Betten, Richard Harrison, and Sal Mamusia, 1991.

13. Have a Beer with Fear (5.11b, 50 feet, sport) This line is found a few feet to the right of Caustic on the less defined arête. The route feels like two boulder problems stacked on top of one another. 4 bolts. **FA:** Paul Van Betten and Richard Harrison, 1992.

14. Fear This (5.11c, 40 feet, sport) Just to the right of Have a Beer with Fear, easy terrain leads to a cruxy bulge. One online commenter described this as a "six move V3ish boulder problem, followed by runout 5.8 to the anchors." 3 bolts. **FA:** Sal Mamusia and Paul Van Betten, 1992.

15. Elbows of Mac and Ronnie (5.11a, 45 feet, sport) Found 10 feet right of Fear This, Elbows of Mac and Ronnie starts at a right-leaning ramp. The climbing eases toward the top. Work up the left side of the flake and onto the face. 4 bolts. **FA:** Todd Swain, 1992.

16. What's Eating You? (5.10a, 45 feet, sport, TR) Found 10 feet right of Elbows of Mac and Ronnie. Climb the left-facing flake up through a bulge. A stick clip or a TCU is recommended to protect the lower part of the route. 3 bolts, small cams. **FA:** Todd Swain and Randy and Andy Schenkel, 1992.

Cannibal Crag

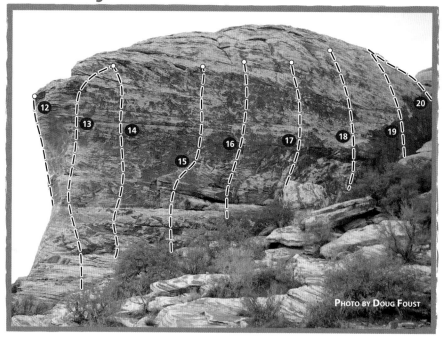

PHOTO BY DOUG FOUST

17. A Man in Every Pot (5.8+, 45 feet, sport, TR) Start at the large white flake leaning against the face and crank straight up to the anchors. 3 bolts. **FA:** Debbie Brenchley and Todd Swain, 1992.

18. Mac and Ronnie in Cheese (5.10a, 40, sport, TR) This line starts 3 feet right of a large flake leaning against the wall. Climb up past four bolts to the top. 4 bolts. **FA:** Debbie Brenchley and Todd Swain, 1992.

19. Ma and Pa in the Kettle (5.7, 30 feet, mixed, TR) This climb is found on the far right-hand side of the wall. Climb past three bolts to the top. 3 bolts, small cams are helpful. **FA:** Todd Swain, 1992.

20. Shishka Bob (5.6 X, 20 feet, TR) This varnished face, found to the right of Ma and Pa in the Kettle, was originally climbed as a solo ascent. The line is immediately left of the ramp that accesses the top of Cannibal Crag and can be toproped with some creative anchoring. **FA:** Todd Swain, 1992.

RIDING HOOD WALL

Riding Hood Wall is a beautiful piece of rock, pierced by a striking crack, all of which overlooks the entirety of the Calico Basin above Sandstone Drive.

Physical Graffiti was one of a young Randal Grandstaff's early first ascents in Red Rock. The iconic climbing guide helped establish this line in 1973 and went on to be a major player in the development of new climbs in the conservation area.

The wall fell out of favor for a time, and the only people who ever seemed to be on it were climbing guides. However, in 2011 Dan Young established what has become the most popular multi-pitch line in the canyon. Big Bad Wolf brought hordes of moderate sport climbers up the wall. And the popularity of the route inevitably created lines at the base, which also—inevitably—caused some to explore the adjacent classic. The result is that Physical Graffiti has seen a well-deserved renaissance of climbers jamming their way up the classic route.

Approach: Park at the Red Springs parking area or at the Elbow. From Red Springs take one of the trails from the right-hand side of the parking lot toward Cannibal Crag. Continue under Cannibal Crag and toward the large obvious wall. Cut up a steep gully and make a traversing approach toward the base of the wall. Expect some 2nd- and 3rd-class scrambling on the approach. **Time:** 20 to 30 minutes.

Sun Exposure: Riding Hood Wall receives morning sun and afternoon shade.

Types of Climbing Available: Trad, sport, multi-pitch, face and crack climbing

1. Big Bad Wolf (5.9, II, 220 feet, sport) This line is found approximately 30 feet up and to the left of Physical Graffiti above a flat sloping rock. (Heavy rainstorms in 2015 moved this rock from directly beneath the route approximately 5 feet down the gully.) The route requires eight quickdraws to complete in four pitches. Pitches 1 and 2 or 2 and 3 can be combined with seventeen draws. **Pitch 1:** Climb up the jug haul to the first anchor (5.9, 70 feet). **Pitch 2:** Continue up, working through the crux approximately halfway through the pitch, to the next set of anchors (5.8, 70 feet). **Pitch 3:** Work from the slab up through steeper terrain to the next anchor (5.8, 70 feet). **Pitch 4:** Scramble up easy terrain, passing two bolts to the top of the wall. Be sure to clip each bolt to avoid knocking loose rock down on people below (5.0, 30 feet). **Note:** Please do not rappel this route. It is far better to use the Riding Hood Wall walk-off to avoid problems with parties below. **FA:** Dan Young, Lynda Gallia, and Evan Allen, 2011.

Riding Hood Wall

2. Physical Graffiti (5.7, II, 300 feet, trad) **Pitch 1:** Ascend the obvious crack system up steep dark rock and belay at the comfortable double-bolt belay station (5.6, 100 feet). **Pitch 2:** Climb the crack system up and to the right. The crux of the route is only a few feet above the belay. After approximately 160 feet the crack will begin to diminish, and it will become somewhat ledgey. As you top out, note that there are two possible places for an anchor. The lower potential anchor includes a number of small horizontal cracks. The higher potential anchor requires larger gear, but also includes a better ledge to stand on (5.7, 180–190 feet). **Note:**

It is hard to hear your partner if this route is done in the classic two-pitch fashion. For better communication, consider breaking the route into three pitches. Pro to 3 inches. **FA:** Jon Martinet, Randal Grandstaff, and Scott Gordon, 1973.

3. Over the Hill to Grandma's House (5.9+, II, 300 feet, trad) This line climbs up the crack system to the right of Physical Graffiti. The triangular roof easily identifies it, as the roof has crack options on both the right and left sides. At first glance the left side appears to be longer, but it is the easier of the two options. Continue up the crack to the Physical Graffiti anchors and then either finish on Physical Graffiti or make a 100-foot rappel back to the ground. **FA:** Bob Logerquist and John Williamson, 1970.

Riding Hood Wall Descent: The easiest option is to scramble off to the left (see topo). From the top of Physical Graffiti, there are a few exposed moves in the corner. After that you'll meet up with the top of Big Bad Wolf. Once off the Riding Hood Wall, follow a trail to a notch, from which the First Pullout is visible. Descend the slightly steep gully behind the tree and work back around to the base of the route. **Note:** Do not rappel Big Bad Wolf, as commonly there are people below.

COWLICK CRAG

This beautiful little crag provides lots of options for beginner and intermediate climbers. There are toprope routes and sport climbs, an easy approach, and sunny climbing. And indeed, the Cowlick Crag is one of the best crags in the conservation area for children. The crag provides easy toprope access and a flat base with no exposure.

Approach: Park at the Red Springs Picnic Area. From there, approach as if for Cannibal Crag by taking one of the trails to the right of the boardwalk. Continue on the trail as it cuts under Cannibal Crag and curves to the west. Approximately 10 minutes from the parking lot, you'll

1. Happy Acres
2. Cut Your Teeth Crag
3. Cowlick Crag
4. Approach Gully for The Fox

be moving up the drainage under the Riding Hood Wall, heading straight toward the low notch in the Calico Hills. Continue on the main trail for another 5 minutes or so until the blob of the Cowlick Crag appears on the right-hand side. If you start to walk uphill toward the notch, you've gone too far. **Time:** 20 minutes.

Sun Exposure: Cowlick Crag is in the sun all day.

Types of Climbing Available: Toprope, sport, face climbing

1. Bedhead (5.6, 50 feet, TR) Found on the south side of the feature in the gully, this line is a fun beginner climb. Access to the toprope anchor is mildly exposed. There is a belay

bolt at the top of the crag that may be used to safely reach the bolts. **FA:** Mark Limage.

2. HeadBed (5.5, 50 feet, TR) Found just to the right of Bedhead, this is another excellent beginner climb. Use the belay bolt to access the anchors. **FA:** Mark Limage.

3. Pancakes and Porn (5.8, 80 feet, TR) This toprope, found just left of Cowlick Co. Crag, climbs right through the middle of the roof. Some of the rock is a bit loose here. **FA:** Jason Martin, 2007.

4. Cowlick Co. Crag (5.7, 80 feet, sport, TR) The central route on the

Cowlick Crag

main face was the first to be established on the rock. It's a little runout by most gym climber standards. Climb past four bolts to the anchor. The route may be toproped from the summit of the crag. However, if rope drag is an issue, rappel from the top and set up the toprope on the lower anchors. 4 bolts. **FA:** Todd and Donette Swain and Mike Dimitri, 1993.

5. Flying Chuckwalla (5.7, 60 feet, sport, TR) The next sport climb on the wall is found just to the right of Cowlick Co. Crag. And like that route, the line may be toproped from the top of the crag. 4 bolts. **FA:** Mark Limage and Dave Melchoir, 2000.

6. Bad Hair Day (5.7, 40 feet, TR) The anchor for this route is found just down and right of those for Flying Chuckwalla. Scramble down into the notch to find the toprope bolts. **FA:** Mark Limage.

7. The Wonderful World of Shrimpy (5.7, 50 feet, TR) The author and his wife referred to their as yet unborn child as Shrimpy when he put up this and the next route. To the right of the notch is a small tower. A set of bolts are found on the summit of the feature. The first line on the tower climbs directly up and left of the overhang. **FA:** Jason Martin, 2007.

8. No Cocktails for Shrimpy (5.6, 50 feet, TR) Climb the face/arête a few feet to the right of The Wonderful World of Shrimpy. Ascend the face to a left-leaning crack, then join the anchors for The Wonderful World. **FA:** Jason Martin, 2007.

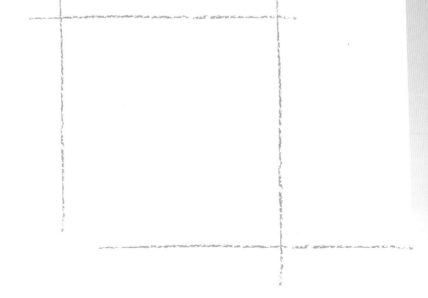

THE FOX WALL
What does the fox say?
This question is easily answered when you're under the Fox Wall. It says lots of loud swear words, intermixed with a little bit of screaming and occasionally some crying. The Fox is an awesome route, but for the standard Red Rock climber who's used to climbing the face and protecting the crack, it is a hard climb.

The Fox Wall has been the site of several rope solo accidents and rappelling accidents. If you elect to

The Fox Wall

1 is around corner to the left

2

rappel, be sure that your ropes touch down before descending. The wall is taller than you think.

Approach: From the Red Springs Picnic Area, follow trails to the northwest. Pass Cannibal Crag and Riding Hood Wall and continue until almost at Cowlick Crag. About 10 minutes up the hill above the trail is a beautiful right-facing corner. Scramble up to the base of this to get to the wall. **Time:** 25 minutes.

Sun Exposure: The Fox Wall receives morning sun and afternoon shade.

Types of Climbing Available: Trad, toprope, steep and pumpy crack climbing

1. The Hound (5.8, 60 feet, trad, TR) This line is up and left of The Fox in the descent gully. Some shenanigans are involved with topping out or setting it up as a toprope. There are a pair of bolts at the top of the crack that may be used for descent or for toproping after a lead. Pro to 4 inches. **FA:** Unknown.

2. The Fox (5.10d, 105 feet, trad, TR) Jam up the splitter crack, working through a couple of offwidth moves to attain the top. To descend, scramble off to the left. **Note:** There have been several accidents at this crag due to the route's length. It's not a bad idea to tie knots at the end of your rappel/toprope ropes. Pro to 5 inches. Most people require doubles in the 2- to 4-inch range. Some bring gear up to the 6-inch range. **FA:** John Williamson and Bob Logerquist, 1970.

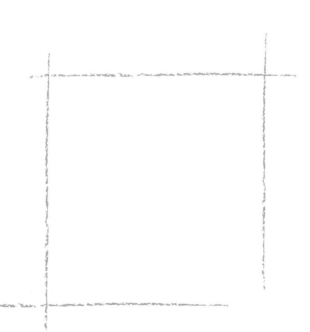

A climber cranks through the offwidth section of The Fox.
PHOTO BY JARED DRAPALA

CUT YOUR TEETH CRAG

Cut Your Teeth Crag is an excellent place for beginner-level sport climbers. The routes are friendly, well protected, and fun.

But a word of caution—this is not a good area for small children. Some of the routes are perched atop a large ledge. Care must be taken at the main wall of the crag.

Approach: From the Red Springs Picnic Area, follow the trail that cuts away to the northwest. Continue on the trail beneath Cannibal Crag and Riding Hood Wall toward the obvious notch. Continue past Cowlick Crag and climb steeply up to the crag found just below the notch on the right-hand side.

The crag is broken into two obvious sections. On the left are two sport routes. In between is a gully, which may be used to access the top of the main wall for toproping. To the right of the gully is the main wall. **Time:** 30 minutes.

Sun Exposure: Cut Your Teeth Crag is exposed to the sun all day. It can also be a very windy place.

Types of Climbing Available: Trad, sport, toprope, moderate face and crack climbing

1. November Daze (5.7, 100 feet, sport) This fun line is found approximately 50 feet to the left of the main wall and just a few feet left of the gully that separates the two features. This bolted line was originally put up on lead, which is a rarity in Red Rock. 9 bolts. **FA:** Mark Limage and Gary Sanders, 2000.

2. September Nights (5.8, 100 feet, sport) This is a tricky little line to the right of November Daze and just left of the "separation gully." 8 bolts. **FA:** Todd Lane and Mike McGlynn, 2006.

3. Interproximal Stripper (5.7, 60 feet, sport, TR) This line is immediately right of the "separation gully" and on the left-hand side of the Cut Your Teeth Crag. Be aware that the line is a little loose. Interproximal Stripper can be toproped by rappelling to the anchors from Braces and Bridges. 7 bolts. **FA:** Todd Lane, 2006.

4. Laughing Gas (5.7, 50 feet, TR) To set up a toprope on this climb, access it from Interproximal Stripper or by rappelling from Braces and Bridges. **FA:** Donny Seablom, 2006.

Cut Your Teeth Crag

5. Braces and Bridges (5.8, 65 feet, TR) Ascend the wall just left of the crack that splits the feature. **FA:** Jory Stiegel, 2006.

6. Toothache (5.6, 45 feet, TR) This toprope is found just right of Braces and Bridges. Some exposed scrambling will bring you to the toprope anchors at the top of the crag. **FA:** Mike McGlynn, 2006.

7. Impacted Molar (5.6, 40 feet, sport, TR) This super-short, super-fun line is found directly to the right of Toothache. There might be some rappelling shenanigans from Toothache to set up a toprope. 4 bolts. **FA:** Mike McGlynn, 2006.

8. Baby Teeth (5.5, 35 feet, trad) On the extreme right-hand side of the wall is a short traditional climb. This is a nice little line for beginner-level leaders. Pro to 3 inches. **FA:** Mike McGlynn, 2006.

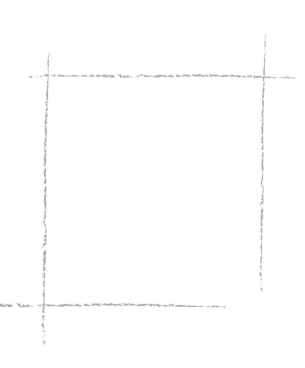

First Pullout

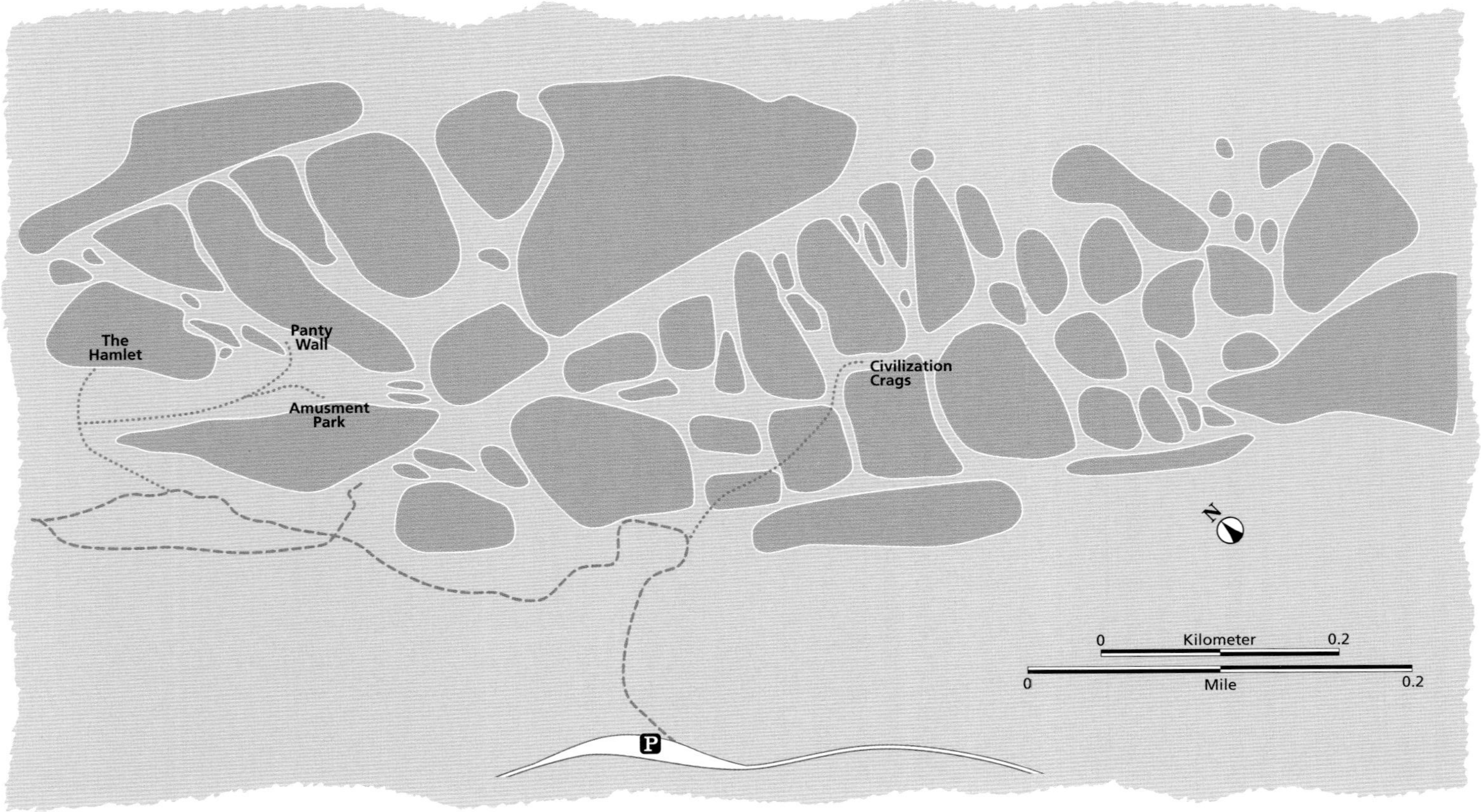

Civilization
Crags

Panty
Wall

Amusment
Park

The
Hamlet

P

N

Kilometer

0   0.2

Mile

0   0.2

2.

First Pullout

As the First Pullout—officially known as Calico I—is the first stop that people can make inside the Red Rock Canyon Scenic Drive, the place can be a bit of a zoo. The climbing here is absolutely awesome, but the parking can be a nightmare. If you arrive before 10 a.m., parking shouldn't be a problem. But if you arrive after that, especially on a weekend, you will be in the thick of it.

Approach: The First Pullout is the first parking area inside the Red Rock Canyon Scenic Drive. At the north end of the parking area, there are a number of slots with signs that indicate they are for "all-day parking." It's important to park there instead of in the short-term parking because overweight tourists, wedding parties, drunk fraternity boys in limos, and scantily clad photo-shoot models don't wish to walk the additional 70 feet to the trailhead. Be considerate of these other visitors; it's part of Leave No Trace.

CIVILIZATION CRAGS

The Civilization Crags provide a number of well-bolted and pleasant sport routes in the 5.9 to 5.10 range. The lines are slightly harder than those found on Panty Wall or The Hamlet, and are more in line with those found in the Black Corridor. Michael Kimm, a Las Vegas–based teacher and actor, envisioned this area in 2010; over the next four years, he bolted and sent all the routes. Michael has been one of the most active moderate sport route developers in the area, and everyone who enjoys this kind of line owes him a beer.

Approach: This approach can be complex, so it's good to spot the crag from the parking lot before making your way to it. The Civilization Crags are southeast of the lot and are most easily identified by the huge northwest-facing, varnished corner.

From the parking lot, drop down the trail into the drainage on the right. Once in the gravel continue until you find a break in the sandstone on the left. Scramble up through broken terrain and make your way south and east to the base of the crag. There is no obvious route, and the best way to get there is to look for the crag every time you're able to get a view of it. Expect lots of 3rd-class scrambling and a few mistakes and dead ends on the approach. **Time:** 20 minutes.

Sun Exposure: The slot and the main wall see limited sun. In the winter there is almost no sun on these aspects. The southwest face sees late morning and afternoon sun.

Types of Climbing Available: Sport and face climbs, primarily in the 5.10 range

There are five areas at the Civilization Crags. The first area is where a single route (The Sun Never Sets) resides. This is up and left of the rest of the crag on a prow. The second area is The Slot, the third is the Main Wall, the fourth is the Southwest Face, and the final area is the Southeast Face.

At the time of this writing, the area sported seventeen climbs!

1. The Sun Never Sets (5.7, 55 feet, sport) This line is up and left of the main area on a prow of rock. 6 bolts. **FA:** Michael Kimm, 2010.

2. Byzantium (5.10b, 45 feet, sport) This line is left of the main wall. It is the left-most route in The Slot. 6 bolts. **FA:** Michael Kimm, 2010.

3. Mongol Hoarde (5.10a, 40 feet, sport) Found to the right of Byzantium, in the center of The Slot, this line

Civilization Crags

climbs up a varnished wall to a small overhang with nice jugs. 5 bolts. **FA:** Michael Kimm, 2010.

4. Ming Dynasty (5.9, 40 feet, sport) This is the right-most line in The Slot. 4 bolts. **FA:** Michael Kimm, 2010.

5. The Fall of Rome (5.10b R, 70 feet, sport) This route is on the left side of the main wall at the tallest point. The line is a bit dangerous, and a stick clip is recommended for the second bolt. Climb through a few hard crimps to easier terrain. 6 bolts. **FA:** Michael Kimm, 2010.

6. Manifest Destiny (5.9+, 70 feet, sport) Found just to the right of The Fall of Rome. Work through a few crimps to the varnished face above. 6 bolts. **FA:** Michael Kimm, 2010.

7. This is Sparta (5.9, 60 feet, sport) Found right of Manifest Destiny, this line works up a chimney and then out onto the face. 5 bolts. **FA:** Michael Kimm, 2010.

8. Babylon 5.8 (5.8, 40 feet, sport) Climb the face right of the chimney. 4 bolts. **FA:** Michael Kimm, 2010.

9. Evil Empire (5.10d, 30 feet, trad) This is the arching crack between Babylon 5.8 and Conquistador. This isn't a true crack climb, but it is a technical line. One large cam (4-plus inches) and then small cams to 0.5 inch are recommended. **FA:** Killis Howard, 2011.

10. Conquistador (5.10d, 30 feet, sport) This route climbs the blank-looking wall on the right-hand side of the main feature. 4 bolts. **FA:** Michael Kimm, 2010.

The following routes continue around the corner and onto the other side of the feature.

11. Meerkat Manor (5.7, 50 feet, trad) Found around the corner, this line climbs the wide crack on the southwest side of the feature. It is possible to climb the crack at 5.7 or climb the easier 5.6 face to the right. Rap off Conquistador to descend. Pro to 4 inches. **FA:** Unknown.

12. East India Trading Company (5.6, 50 feet, sport) This fun little sport climb is found to the right of Meerkat Manor. Work up the slab to big moves and then back to the slab. 5 bolts. **FA:** Michael Kimm, 2014.

13. The Three Kingdoms (5.7, 70 feet, sport) This line climbs the highest point on the southwest face. 8 bolts. **FA:** Michael Kimm, 2014.

14. Super Tsardom (5.4, 60 feet, sport) A blunt arête defines the separation between the southwest and southeast faces. Super Tsardom sends this feature. 6 bolts. **FA:** Michael Kimm, 2014.

15. Five Charter Oath (5.8, 55 feet, sport) Found right of Super Tsardom. Climb up the steep wall through large jugs to a small roof. Pull the roof and finish the line. 7 bolts. **FA:** Michael Kimm, 2014.

16. Sultans and Viziers (5.8+, 55 feet, sport) This line climbs up steep terrain through a roof to a shared anchor with Five Charter Oath. 6 bolts. **FA:** Michael Kimm, 2014.

17. Umayyad Caliphate (5.9+, 60 feet, sport) This is the right-most route on the southeast face. 7 bolts. **FA:** Michael Kimm, 2014.

THE HAMLET

The Hamlet is the best beginner sport crag in the conservation area. This is a bold statement, but it's true. The lines are generally tightly bolted and friendly. And the climbing is fun! Fun! Fun!

Approach: Park at the First Pullout in the all-day parking area. Drop down the main trail. At the fork follow the left-hand path, which drops down into the drainage. Continue on the main trail up a short, steep hill. From the top of the hill, continue left until a faint trail drops down to the right on a 2nd- and 3rd-class ramp into a brushy drainage. Follow the trail, working across the drainage and up onto an area of broken red rock. Make a U-turn here and start to climb up the ramp toward the Panty Wall. The Hamlet is the wall on the left-hand side of the ramp. **Time:** 10 minutes.

Sun Exposure: This wall gets sun from mid-morning until the sun goes down. The bases of some routes are in a small gully, which can protect from afternoon sun.

Types of Climbing Available: Sport, toprope, face climbing The Hamlet is composed of two tiers, the Lower Hamlet and the Upper Hamlet. The left side of the Lower Hamlet has also been called The J-Wall due to rock discoloration in the shape of a "J." All the routes at the Lower Hamlet are easily toproped.

The right-hand side of the Lower Hamlet has cleaned up quite a bit over the last few years, but there is still some rockfall potential. Helmets are advised, and belayers should stand well away from the base of the wall.

Lower Hamlet
1. The J-Wall (5.12b, 40 feet, sport, TR) This is the first route on the lower tier of The Hamlet. A bouldery move at the base leads to easier climbing. 4 bolts. **FA:** Unknown.

2. Killer Joe (5.10c, 50 feet, sport, TR) Send the line right of The J-Wall. The direct start is 5.12. 5 bolts. **FA:** Unknown.

3. Mind If I Do a J? (5.10a, 55 feet, sport, TR) This is the right-most of the "J-Trilogy." The line starts up patina, passing five bolts to chains. 5 bolts. **FA:** Unknown.

4. Undiscovered Country (5.7, 85 feet, TR) Undiscovered Country is the first of four toprope lines on the lower tier of The Hamlet. These are all easily reached by scrambling up the ramp on the left. There have been some problems with people stealing hangers atop these routes. There are currently three sets of glue-ins above the wall. This first line is just right of a blank section of rock, on the left-hand side of the large flake/shield. **FA:** Jason Martin, 2007.

5. What Dreams May Come (5.6, 85 feet, TR) Crank up the center of the flake/shield feature to easier climbing above. **FA:** Jason Martin, 2007.

6. The Madness and the Method (5.8, 85 feet, TR) Climb through the tricky roof on the right side of the flake/shield feature. If you cheat through the left side of the steep moves, the line is 5.7. **FA:** Jason Martin, 2007.

7. The Rest Is Silence (5.8, 85 feet, TR) The final of the toprope routes listed here is the best of the toprope routes listed here. Climb just right of the roof on the flake feature to easier climbing. **FA:** Jason Martin, 2007.

Upper Hamlet
8. The Play's the Thing (5.5, 60 feet, sport, TR) This is the left-most route on the upper Hamlet wall, just left of the arch. Belayers should clip into the bolt at the base so they don't tumble down into the bushes below. Climb the low-angle slab to an anchor. It's possible to toprope this route by scrambling up the zigzag ramp. 3 bolts. **FA:** Phil Bridgers and Jason Martin, 2008.

9. The Die Is Cast (5.9, 85 feet, sport) This line starts under the small roof at Upper Hamlet. The crux is the roof move, and then the rest easier. 5 bolts. **FA:** Doug Dye and Thomas Beck, 2015.

The Hamlet

10. Frailty, Thy Name Is Sandstone
(5.7, 85 feet, sport) This juggy line is
found just right of the arch. 8 bolts.
FA: Phil Bridgers, Jason Martin, and
Viren and Julie Perumal, 2008.

11. Sweets to the Sweet (5.7, 85
feet, sport) Just right of Frailty, this is
a sweet climb with sweet holds and
a sweet ledge at the top. 8 bolts. **FA:**
Jason Martin and Phil Bridgers, 2008.

12. When the Blood Burns (5.8+,
85 feet, sport, TR) Originally designed
as a toprope-only route, this line was
bolted in 2016 and provides another
nice sport lead. Found just to the
right of Sweets to the Sweet, it was
originally 5.10a. After a lot of ascents
and a lot of sandy holds broken away,
it feels a lot more like 5.8. Crank
through the roof to easier terrain
above. 7 bolts. **FA:** Phil Bridgers and
Jason Martin, 2008.

13. To Grunt and Sweat (5.8, 60 feet,
sport) This is the first bolted line in the
slot corridor, right of When the Blood
Burns. Climb through the low crux to
easier terrain above. **FA:** Andy Reger
and Dan Young, 2013.

14. Perchance to Dream (5.8, 90
feet, sport) The second bolted line
in the corridor. Blast up through
another low crux to easier climbing
above. 9 bolts. **FA:** Andy Reger and
Dan Young, 2013.

15. Sea of Troubles (5.9, 90 feet,
sport) Start in the chimney behind
the lower tier. Easy terrain leads to a
steep bulge. Crank through the crux
and clip the last link in the chain to
protect from a ledge fall. 9 bolts. **FA:**
Phil Bridgers, Jason Martin, and Julie
and Viren Perumal, 2008.

16. Rosencrantz (5.6, 85 feet, sport)
Climb up past the toprope anchors
above the lower tier to the end of the
ramp. Make a 3rd-class move to the
belay anchor, then follow brown bolts
up to an anchor at a small stance. Be
very careful rappelling or lowering
back to the anchor—knots at the end
of your rope are recommended. Note
that the bottom anchors can be used
to toprope the line below at approximately 5.9. 6 bolts. **FA:** John Wilder
and Scott Massey, 2011.

17. Guildenstern (5.5, 90 feet, sport)
This is the right-most route on the
Hamlet wall. To the right of Rosencrantz is another set of belay bolts.
A 3rd-class move or two will provide
access to these. Climb up and right
toward the arête, clipping a line of
tan bolts. Be very careful rappelling
or lowering back to the anchor—
knots at the end of your rope are
recommended. 8 bolts. **FA:** Scott
Massey, 2011.

PANTY WALL

Ahhh, the Panty Wall. This is perhaps the most popular beginner and intermediate wall in the conservation area. With well over one hundred days of climbing and guiding there, I've had some great times on that wall. I've also had some not so great times.

In 2007 I rappelled off the end of my rope at the Panty Wall and fractured my pelvis. The rope ends were offset, and I didn't have knots in the end of the rope. I got lucky, recovered, and returned to climbing and guiding.

A few years earlier another local guide was working at that wall when something similar happened. He suffered open fractures in both ankles. He got lucky, recovered, and returned to climbing and guiding.

But not everyone is so lucky. The moral of the story is that you should always have knots in the end of your rope, in both single- and multi-pitch terrain. There's simply no reason not to. And indeed, easy to moderate climbing on a fun little beginner crag might be the most dangerous kind. It's the kind that allows climbers to drop their guard.

Approach: Park at the First Pullout in the all-day parking area. Drop down the main trail. At the fork follow the left-hand path, which drops down into the drainage. Continue on the main trail up a short, steep hill. From the top of the trail, go left until a faint trail drops down to the right on a 2nd- and 3rd-class ramp into a brushy drainage. Follow the trail working across the drainage and up onto a broken red rock area. Make a U-turn here and start to climb the ramp, passing The Hamlet and heading toward the large varnished wall that looks a little bit like a large black, inverted triangle . . . or a pair of panties, depending on your perspective. The first route listed here is almost directly behind the broken tree. **Time:** 15 minutes.

Sun Exposure: The Panty Wall is in the sun from late morning through late afternoon.

Types of Climbing Available: Trad, sport, toprope, face and crack climbing

1. Panty Raid (5.10a, 70 feet, trad) Climb up through steep varnished rock, passing a single crux move to a pair of chains. Pro to 1.5 inches. **FA:** Paul Van Betten and Nick Nordblom, 1987.

2. Panty Line (5.10a, 70 feet, trad) Climb the line 5 feet to the right of Panty Raid. Use the anchors for that route. Pro to 1.5 inches. **FA:** Paul Van Betten and Nick Nordblom, 1987.

3. Undies (5.8, 70 feet, TR) This toprope is just up and left of the anchors for Brief Encounter. Climb Brief Encounter to set up the line. **FA:** Unknown.

Panty Wall

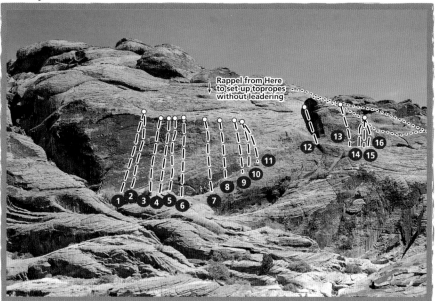

Rappel from Here
to set-up topropes
without leadering

4. Brief Encounter (5.8, 70 feet, sport) This is the first of the sport climbs on the left side of the main wall. 6 bolts. **FA:** Leo Henson and Albert Newman, 1998.

5. Sacred Undergarment Squeeze Job (5.8, 65 feet, sport) The line is squeezed between Brief Encounter and Boxer Rebellion, but isn't really a "squeeze job." The line is too much fun. 6 bolts. **FA:** Mark Limage, 2004.

6. Boxer Rebellion (5.8, 65 feet, sport) Just right of Sacred Undergarment, climb through the low crux to easier terrain. 6 bolts. **FA:** Leo Henson and Albert Newman, 1996.

7. Black Lace (5.8, 65 feet, sport) Found immediately right of Boxer Rebellion, but before the ramp. Blast up past three bolts to a crux at the fourth bolt. Continue up past three more bolts to the anchor. **FA:** Lynda Gallia and Dan Young, 2013.

8. The Last Panty (5.7, 50 feet, sport) The next route to the right climbs slabby holds. Be aware of the drop-off that threatens the belayer. The last bolt before the anchor provides some easy but runout climbing. 6 bolts. **FA:** Unknown.

9. Silk Panties (5.7, 45 feet, sport) The farthest bolted route to the right is found at the top of the ramp. 5 bolts. **FA:** Todd and Donette Swain, 1994.

10. Panty Loon (5.8, 45 feet, TR) Immediately to the right of the Silk Panties anchor, there is a second anchor. Use this anchor to toprope this route and Scanty Panty. **FA:** B. Binder and Em Holland, 2001.

11. Scanty Panty (5.7, 40 feet, TR) Climb the choss just to the right of Panty Loon. **FA:** Todd and Donette Swain, 1994.

12. Cover My Buttress (5.5, 35 feet, trad, TR) A nice short crack is found in the left-facing corner on the right-hand side of the Panty Wall. This makes for a good beginner trad lead. Gear to 3 inches. **FA:** Todd Swain, 1994.

13. Butt Floss (5.8–5.10a, 35 feet, TR) This line, found to the right of Cover My Buttress, climbs just right of a low roof. The route may be toproped by walking around to the right. The toprope bolts are slightly over the lip; take appropriate cautions when setting it up. **FA:** Unknown.

14. Thong (5.7, 35 feet, trad, TR) Found a few feet right of Butt Floss, this line sends the seam up to the bolted anchors. Gear to 1.5 inches. **FA:** Todd Swain and Marion Parker, 1994.

15. Tighty Whities (5.7+, 30 feet, TR) Climb straight up the toprope line to the anchors for Thong. **FA:** Unknown.

16. Granny Panties (5.6, 30 feet, TR) Start at the short arching crack and climb through the varnish to the anchors for Thong. **FA:** Unknown.

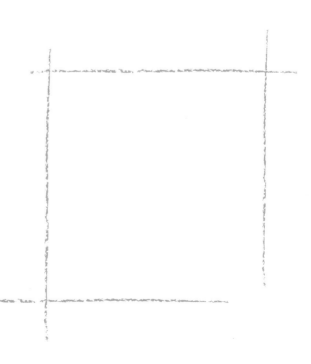

AMUSEMENT PARK

Amusement Park is another excellent beginner sport and toprope crag. But this really isn't a good place for intermediates, as it might be a little too easy. That said, this is also a great crag for children; the routes are short and shaded, and there are few places for unsupervised kids to fall off anything.

Approach: Park at the First Pullout in the all-day parking area. Drop down the main trail. At the fork follow the left-hand path, which drops down into the drainage. Continue on the main trail up a short, steep hill. From the top of the trail, go left until a faint trail drops down to the right on a 2nd- and 3rd-class ramp into a brushy drainage. Follow the trail working across the drainage and up onto a broken red rock area. Make a U-turn here and start to climb the ramp, passing The Hamlet and heading toward the Panty Wall. Amusement Park is directly below and facing the Panty Wall. **Time:** 15 minutes.

Sun Exposure: This crag sees morning sun and then is in the shade throughout the afternoon.

Types of Climbing Available: Easy toproping and sport climbing There are four hook anchors at the top of the wall. Each of the nine lines goes to one of these anchors. You can easily scramble around to set up topropes on all of these lines.

1. Power Tower (5.7, 35 feet, sport, TR) This left-most line starts near the chimney. 4 bolts. **FA:** Lynda Gallia and Dan Young, 2014.

2. Bumper Cars (5.7, 35 feet, sport, TR) This second route from the left shares an anchor with Power Tower. 4 bolts. **FA:** Lynda Gallia and Dan Young, 2014.

3. Demon Drop (5.7, 35 feet, sport, TR) The third route from the left. 4 bolts. **FA:** Lynda Gallia and Dan Young, 2014.

4. Haunted House (5.7, 35 feet, sport, TR) The fourth route from the left shares an anchor with Demon Drop. It's possible to make a slabby start or to traverse into the first bolt. 4 bolts. **FA:** Lynda Gallia and Dan Young, 2014.

5. Cotton Candy (5.7, 35 feet, TR) This fifth route from the left is a toprope only. Set up the rope on Log Flume to climb this line. **FA:** Lynda Gallia and Dan Young, 2014.

6. Log Flume (5.7, 35 feet, sport, TR) This line is in the middle of the wall. It is the sixth climbing line and the fifth bolted line from the left. 4 bolts. **FA:** Lynda Gallia and Dan Young, 2014.

Amusement Park

7. Tea Cups (5.7, 35 feet, mixed, TR) This is the sixth bolted line from the left, and it shares an anchor with Tilt-A-Whirl and Roller Coaster. This is the best line on the wall. 4 bolts. **FA:** Lynda Gallia and Dan Young, 2014.

8. Tilt-A-Whirl (5.7, 35 feet, TR) This toprope is on the right-hand side of the wall. Use the anchors for Tea Cups and Roller Coaster. Climb up through the slab, or traverse in from the ledge above the slab to send the line. **FA:** Lynda Gallia and Dan Young, 2014.

9. Roller Coaster (5.7, 35 feet, sport, TR) This is the right-most bolted climbing line. 3 bolts. **FA:** Lynda Gallia and Dan Young, 2014.

3.

The Second Pullout

The Second Pullout is officially known as Calico II. Parking here is limited, so it's important to arrive early. It's not uncommon for dozens of cars to park along the side of the road before and after this parking lot.

Approach: Enter the Red Rock Canyon Scenic Drive and make your way to the second small parking area on the right. There are a lot fewer tourists than at the First Pullout, and a lot more climbers. Plan accordingly.

BLACK CORRIDOR

The Black Corridor provides the most 5.10 to 5.11 bolted lines in any one area anywhere in Red Rock Canyon. There are so many routes in that "kinda-hard" grade that it often feels like an outdoor rock gym. The result is twofold. First, the place is crazy fun. And second, it's also crazy busy.

Approach: Park in the Second Pullout, drop down into the drainage, and follow it upstream. Enter a small

Black Corridor

Climb up through the small canyon with tiered stagnant pools to reach the Black Corridor.

13

The Second Pullout

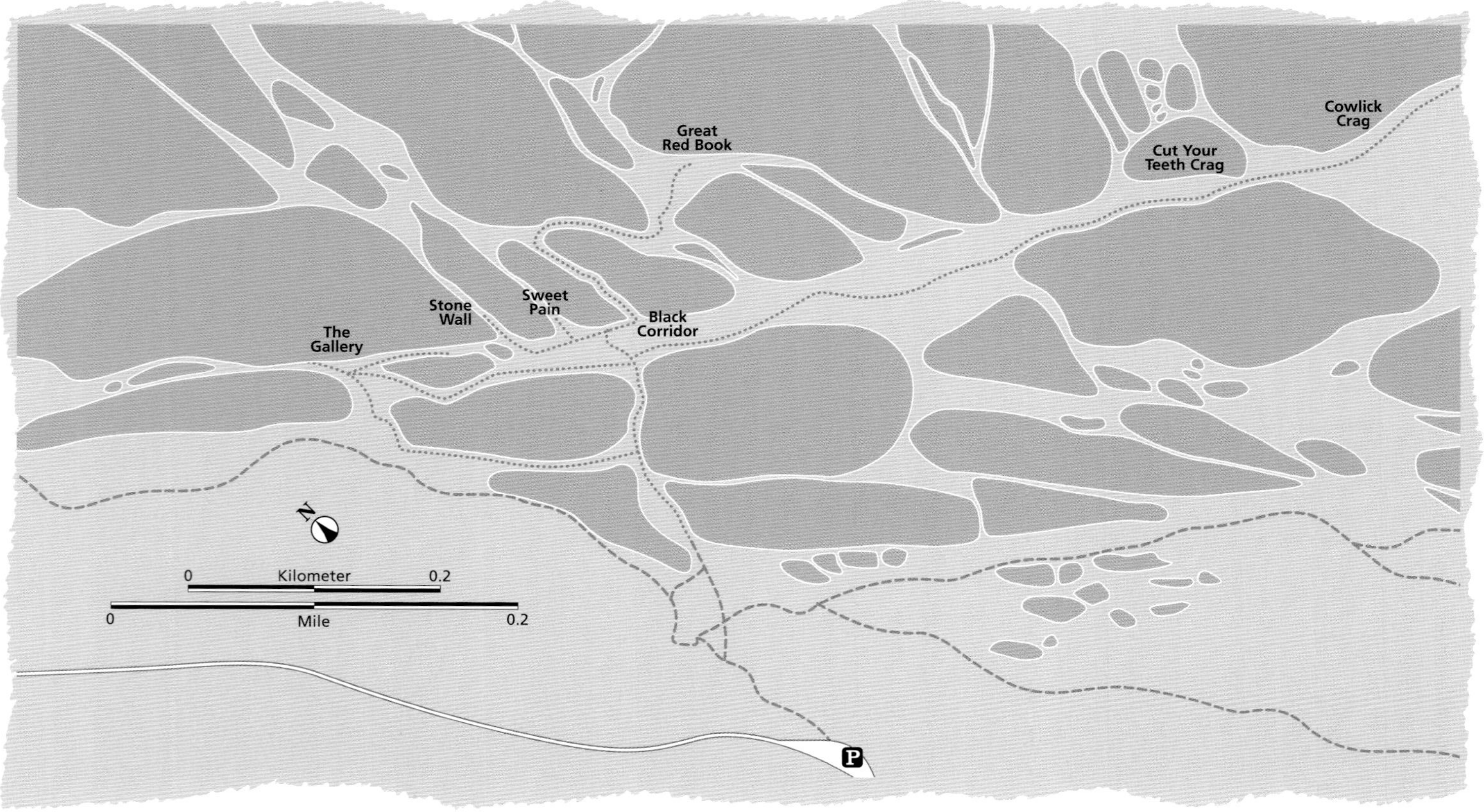

Cowlick Crag

Cut Your Teeth Crag

Great Red Book

Black Corridor

Sweet Pain

Stone Wall

The Gallery

N

Kilometer
0   0.2   0.2

Mile
0   0.2

P

canyon with tiered stagnant pools of water. Climb up on the left side of the pools, making a 4th-class move up a step. Continue up to a sandy shelf. Walk straight from the terminus of the streambed to a wall with a small gully beneath it. Turn right and scramble along the right-hand side of this minor gully. A tree that smells strongly of urine lies at the end of the gully and marks the start of the Black Corridor. **Time:** 15 minutes.

Sun Exposure: There is always shade in the Black Corridor. The area only really sees full sun for about an hour a day and can be cold in the winter.

Types of Climbing Available: Sport, face climbing, some steep climbing

Lower Level—Left Side

1. The CEL (5.9, 60 feet, sport) As you enter the Black Corridor, this is the first bolted route on the left side. A stick clip is good. There have been injuries on this route. 8 bolts. **FA:** Todd Lane, 2006.

2. L2 (5.9+, 50 feet, sport) This second route on the left side is a little runout and a bit more heady than many of the other routes in the Black Corridor. 5 bolts. **FA:** Michelle Locatelli and Lisa Harrison, 2010.

3. L3 (5.9+, 60 feet, sport) The third route on the left-hand side requires some thoughtful movement. **FA:** Unknown, 2010.

4. Bonaire (5.9, 65 feet, sport) The fourth route on the left-hand side. The route is easier when the first few moves are navigated significantly to the right of the first bolt. The line clocks in at 5.10 via the direct approach. 6 bolts. **FA:** Jim Steagall, Kevin Sandefur, Chris Werner, and Dave Sobocan, 1990.

5. Bon Ez (5.9+, 60 feet, sport) The fifth route on the left. 7 bolts. **FA:** Jim Steagall, Kevin Sandefur, Chris Werner, and Dave Sobocan, 1990.

6. Crude Boys (5.10d, 60 feet, sport) The sixth route on the left-hand side. If you climb left after the second bolt, the line is a bit easier. Straight up is harder than 5.10d. 5 bolts. **FA:** Jim Steagall, Kevin Sandefur, Chris Werner, and Dave Sobocan, 1990.

7. Luthier (5.11a, 60 feet, sport) The seventh route on the left side. Beware that this route is a bit weird. You have to clip at least one bolt high on Crude Boys and away from the natural line. Mike McGlynn—a well-known Las Vegas climber, guitar-maker, wood-worker, and great guy—died in an accident on this previously unnamed route in 2007. 5 bolts. **FA:** Unknown.

8. That Black Corridor Mixed Route (5.10d R, 80 feet, mixed) This mixed line to the right of Luthier is a bit thin. Climb up the seam to a bolt and then continue to the top. Gear to 3 inches.

Black Corridor

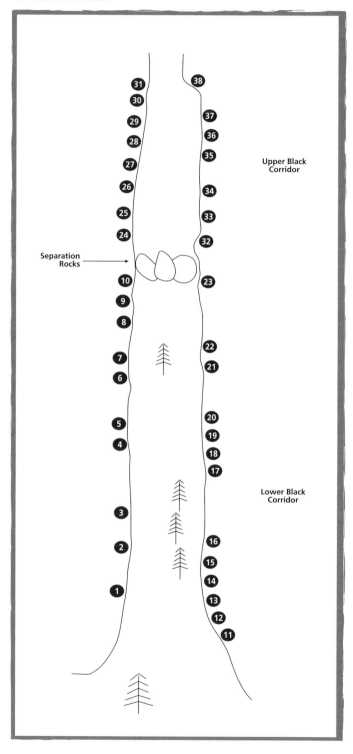

FA: Jim Steagull, Kevin Sandefur, Chris Werner, and Dave Sobocan, 1990.

9. Vagabonds (5.10a, 65 feet, sport) Found just a few feet before the step to the upper level, Vagabonds is the ninth route on the left-hand side. 9 bolts. **FA:** Jim Steagull, Kevin Sandefur, Chris Werner, and Dave Sobocan, 1990.

10. Crude Control (5.12a, 60 feet, sport) The final route on the left side is seldom climbed. 7 bolts. **FA:** Jim Steagull, Kevin Sandefur, Chris Werner, and Dave Sobocan, 1990.

Lower Level—Right Side

11. Adoption (5.11b, 80 feet, sport) Found at the entrance to the Black Corridor, this is the very first climb on the right-hand side. 6 bolts. **FA:** Leo and Karin Henson, 1991.

12. Burros Don't Gamble (5.10c, 80 feet, sport) The second climb on the right-hand side has a spooky start, as there is a bit of groundfall potential. The route eases after the low crux. This route and Burros Might Fly are out of character for the Black Corridor, as they receive afternoon sun. 7 bolts. **FA:** Harrison Shull and Todd Hewitt, 1994.

13. Burros Might Fly (5.10b, 70 feet, sport) The third route on the right-hand side of the Corridor. 7 bolts. **FA:** Harrison Shull and Todd Hewitt, 1994.

14. Psychobilly (5.11a, 60 feet, sport) Found just left of the preceding route. 7 bolts. **FA:** Richard Harrison, 2006.

15. Michael Angelo (5.11b, 60 feet, sport) This line starts right behind a small tree on the right-hand side of the Black Corridor. The first bolt is painted. **FA:** Michelle Locatelli, 2006.

16. M&M (5.11a, 75 feet, sport) This sixth route on the right-hand side of the lower tier is found between two trees above a deep hole in the rock. It gets a bit cruxy between the third and fourth bolts. 7 bolts. **FA:** Dan Meyers and Rob Mansfield, 2007.

17. She's Deadly (5.11a, 70 feet, sport) This line is the seventh on the right-hand side. Follow good movement on huecos to a tough sequence on angling crimps to pull the lip. **FA:** Richard Harrison, Lisa Harrison, and Michelle Locatelli, 2007.

18. The Heavy Hitter (5.10c, 60 feet, sport) This route was likely named after an annoying—but popular—series of Las Vegas television commercials for an attorney who called himself a heavy hitter. The eighth route on the right has two cruxes, a tricky sequence at the bottom, and some large huecos at the top. 8 bolts. **FA:** Mike Moore, 2006.

19. Punch Drunk (5.11c, 50 feet, sport) The next route on the right-hand side climbs a small seam. There are two cruxes, the second being the harder. 8 bolts. **FA:** Mike Moore, 2006.

20. Nightmare on Crude Street (5.10d, 60 feet, sport) Considered one of the best routes on the lower tier, this line is directly across from Bon Ez. 6 bolts. **FA:** Jim Steagull, Kevin Sandefur, Chris Werner, and Dave Sobocan, 1990.

21. Foe (5.11a, 40 feet, sport) Easy jugs lead to a really cool bulge. 5 bolts. **FA:** Richard Harrison, 2006.

22. Friend (5.10d, 40 feet, sport) The twelfth route on the right-hand side. Lots of big holds and lots of big rests. 8 bolts. **FA:** Richard Harrison, 2006.

23. Idiot Parade (5.10c, 40 feet, sport) The final route on the right-hand side is a pumpy little climb. Look for the kneebar! 4 bolts. **FA:** Mike Moore, 2006.

Upper Level—Left Side

24. Thermal Breakdown (5.9+, 50 feet, sport) This is the first route on the upper tier on the left-hand side. A 5.9 on the upper level feels a bit harder than on the lower level. A stick clip might be a good idea for those climbing at their limit. 6 bolts. **FA:** Jim Steagull, Kevin Sandefur, Chris Werner, and Dave Sobocan, 1990.

25. Crude Street Blues (5.9+, 50 feet, sport) The second route on the left side. 5 bolts. **FA:** Jim Steagull, Kevin Sandefur, Chris Werner, and Dave Sobocan, 1990.

26. Crude Behavior (5.9+, 50 feet, sport) The third route on the left-hand side climbs through some cool scoops and huecos. 4 bolts. **FA:** Jim Steagull, Kevin Sandefur, Chris Werner, and Dave Sobocan, 1990.

27. Dancin' with a God (5.10a, 50 feet, sport) The fourth route on the left is as fun as dancing with a god! 6 bolts. **FA:** Jim Steagull, Kevin Sandefur, Chris Werner, and Dave Sobocan, 1990.

28. Live Fast, Die Young (5.10d, 50 feet, sport) The fifth route on the left has a very difficult start, which eases as you continue up. 5 bolts. **FA:** Jim Steagull, Kevin Sandefur, Chris Werner, and Dave Sobocan, 1990.

29. Black Gold (5.10b, 50 feet, sport) A stick clip is recommended for the sixth route on the left. This is a tricky route for shorties. 5 bolts. **FA:** Jim Steagull, Kevin Sandefur, Chris Werner, and Dave Sobocan, 1990.

30. Texas Tea (5.10a, 50 feet, sport) Some thin moves and lots of variety make the seventh route on the left an engaging climb. 5 bolts. **FA:** Jim Steagull, Kevin Sandefur, Chris Werner, and Dave Sobocan, 1990.

31. Fool's Gold (5.10b, 50 feet, sport) The final route on the upper left-hand side starts at the same point as Texas Tea. Climb through the crux right after the first bolt to easier climbing above. 5 bolts. **FA:** Jim Steagull, Kevin Sandefur, Chris Werner, and Dave Sobocan, 1990.

Upper Level—Right Side
32. 757 2x4 (5.7, 50 feet, sport) The first route on the upper right-hand side is the easiest in the Black Corridor. The name comes from the fact that this is a seven-bolt 5.7, and the first ascensionist used a 2x4 piece of wood to assist while he placed the anchor bolts. Work your way up the right-leaning crack/ramp to the anchors. **FA:** Todd Lane and Mike McGlynn, 2006.

33. Oils Well that Ends Well (5.11b, 50 feet, sport) The second route on the right side in the upper Corridor sports two 5.11 cruxes with lots of 5.10 in between. It is possible to toprope this by climbing 757 2x4. 5 bolts. **FA:** Jim Steagull, Kevin Sandefur, Chris Werner, and Dave Sobocan, 1990.

34. Sandstone Enema (5.11b, 60 feet, sport) The third route on the right side in the upper canyon. 7 bolts. **FA:** Jim Steagull, Kevin Sandefur, Chris Werner, and Dave Sobocan, 1990.

35. Lewd Crude and Misconstrued (5.9+, 60 feet, sport) The fourth route on the right-hand side sports a weird start, with easier climbing above. 6 bolts. **FA:** Jim Steagull, Kevin Sandefur, Chris Werner, and Dave Sobocan, 1990.

36. Texas Lite Sweet (5.11b, 40 feet, sport) The fifth route on the right side is about 10 feet past Lewd Crude and Misconstrued. Send the very thin face to an anchor. 4 bolts. **FA:** Jim Steagull, Kevin Sandefur, Chris Werner, and Dave Sobocan, 1990.

37. Livin' on Borrowed Time (5.11c, 40 feet, sport) The sixth route on the right-hand side of the upper level climbs through slabby varnished rock to a double-bolt anchor. The defining feature of this route is the crescent-shaped hold. 4 bolts. **FA:** Jim Steagull, Kevin Sandefur, Chris Werner, and Dave Sobocan, 1990.

38. Rebel Without a Pause (5.11a, 35 feet, sport) The last route on the right-hand side of the upper level. This overhung line is a popular test-piece for those moving from 5.10 to 5.11, and is one of my personal favorites. 4 bolts. **FA:** Jim Steagull, Kevin Sandefur, Chris Werner, and Dave Sobocan, 1990.

GREAT RED BOOK

The Great Red Book wall sports several routes, but it is the giant defining dihedral that inspires you to scream, "I have to climb that." And you do. It is an awesome route!

Great Red Book is also an important route in the history of Red Rock. It was on this route in 2002 that the iconic Red Rock climbing guide and first ascensionist—Randal Grandstaff—fell to his death in a rappelling accident. It's likely the accident was caused by a heart problem of which Randal was unaware.

Shortly after his death someone scratched "R.G. Our Bro," next to the anchor on the top of the first pitch. This dedication has since been scratched away.

Approach: Park in the Second Pullout, drop down into the drainage, and follow it upstream. Enter a small canyon with tiered stagnant pools of water. Climb up on the left side of the pools, making a 4th-class move up a step. Continue up to a sandy shelf. Walk straight from the terminus of the streambed to a wall with a small gully beneath it. Turn right and scramble along the right-hand side of this minor gully. A tree that smells strongly of urine lies at the end of the gully and marks the start of the Black Corridor. Continue through the Corridor to the end.

Great Red Book

Photo by Doug Foust

Scramble up and right through some bushes and make your way toward the obvious giant dihedral.

Sun Exposure: The Great Red Book sees some sun depending on the time of year, but the dihedral provides shade through a good chunk of the day.

Types of Climbing Available: Mixed trad, crack and face climbing, with a little easy offwidth

1. Great Red Book (5.8, II, 300 feet, trad) **Pitch 1:** There are two options for the first pitch. It's possible to climb cracks in the face about 10 feet left of the corner to the first belay, or it is also possible to climb the crack in the right-facing corner. If you climb the corner, you will eventually have to traverse out onto the face to reach the bolts at the top of the first pitch. The difficulty of the pitch depends on the variation (5.7–5.8, 150 feet). **Pitch 2:** Climb the face, passing two bolts and into a small offwidth/lieback. Continue up into the alcove to an anchor. **Descent:** Drop down right and then make your way down the drainage on climber's left, contouring around the feature and back to the base of the climb. Expect some 3rd- and 4th-class scrambling.

SWEET PAIN

The Sweet Pain wall is incredibly fun. Part of this is because the routes are a bit on the soft side. The pain at the wall is sweet. And the success on a "hard" route is even sweeter!

Approach: Park in the Second Pullout, drop down into the drainage, and follow it upstream. Enter a small canyon with tiered stagnant pools of water. Climb up on the left side of the pools, making a 4th-class move up a step. Continue up to a sandy shelf. Walk left in the sand and then turn right into the first gully that makes its way up the hillside. The Sweet Pain wall is found on the first steep feature on the left-hand side of this gully. **Time:** 15 minutes.

Sun Exposure: Though there are a few hours of sun every day, the overhang on the Sweet Pain wall tends to keep the area cool.

Types of Climbing Available: Steep and pumpy sport climbs

1. Sweet Pain (5.12a, 50 feet, sport) The first route on the left side of the wall is soft for the grade. Many guidebooks and web posts put this at anywhere from 5.11a to 5.11d, but the route was originally rated at 5.12a. As such it makes for a feather in many people's hats, and I wouldn't want to ruin that. 5 bolts. **FA:** Leo Henson and Randy Faulk, 1991.

2. The Gambler (5.11a, 50 feet, sport) The second route from the left was

Sweet Pain

put up as a memorial to John "the Gambler" Rosholt. Climb up through large holds and look for the secret no-hands rest near the third bolt. 6 bolts. **FA:** Michelle Locatelli, Richard Harrison, and Lisa Harrison, 2005.

3. Sour Pain (5.11b, 45 feet, sport) The third route from the left is a bit sandier. 7 bolts. **FA:** Unknown.

4. Glitter Gulch (5.11a, 60 feet, sport) The fourth route on the wall is named after a notorious Vegas strip club. Start left of a ledge and angle up past six bolts to the anchor. **FA:** Dudes from the Rockies, 1991.

5. Slave to the Grind (5.11b, 60 feet, sport) This route starts easy but gets harder as the line steepens. Milk the feet to keep the pump down. The crux is around the third bolt. 6 bolts. **FA:** Unknown, but probably the same dudes as Glitter Gulch, 1991.

6. Sister of Pain (5.11c, 60 feet, sport) Hard moves followed by slabby moves are followed by a rest, which is followed by more sustained, pumpy moves. This is the sixth route from the left. 6 bolts. **FA:** Leo and Karin Henson, 1992.

7. Lee Press On (5.12c, 60 feet, sport) Don't climb in the rain. This route has been damaged when wet and has become harder due to broken holds and sharp crimps. **FA:** Leo and Karin Henson, 1992.

8. Pain in the Neck (5.10b R, 55 feet, sport) The second to last route on the wall provides some pucker. Don't blow the second clip. Start at the right-leaning crack and climb into a bowl. The holds get better as you get higher. The climbing is easier to the right of the first bolt, harder but more secure on the left. Depending on variation the line is 5.10a to 5.10c. 5 bolts. **FA:** Unknown, early 1990s.

9. A-Cute Pain (5.8, 55 feet, mixed) This line is found on the far right-hand side of the cliff. Start approximately 8 feet to the right of Pain in the Neck at a left-facing corner. Blast up, passing a bolt, into the right-leaning crack. Continue beyond the crack up large holds through steeper terrain to the anchor. 3 bolts, trad gear to 2 inches. **FA:** Todd and Donette Swain, 1993.

STONE WALL

The Stone Wall is an awesome little crag. It is made up primarily of 5.10s and 5.11s and seldom has the crowds of The Gallery or the Black Corridor. If the Sweet Pain wall harbors routes that are softly graded, the Stone Wall is exactly the opposite. One online commenter wrote, "Sweet Pain is a bunch of 10s that are rated 11, and Stone Wall is a bunch of 11s that are rated as 10s." This isn't exactly true. The reality is that Stone Wall is more honestly rated than the previous wall.

Approach: Park in the Second Pullout, drop down into the drainage, and follow it upstream. Enter a small canyon with tiered stagnant pools of water. Climb up on the left side of the pools, making a 4th-class move up a step. Continue up to a sandy shelf. Walk left in the sand, passing the first gully (Sweet Pain) that makes its way up the hillside, and continue to the next major gully. Cut up the gully to find the routes on the left-hand side. **Time:** 15 minutes.

Sun Exposure: The wall sees late morning sun and afternoon shade.

Types of Climbing Available: Steep and pumpy sport climbs

1. Purple Haze (5.10d, 50 feet, sport) The first route on the left end of the wall. 6 bolts. **FA:** Don Burroughs and Alan Busby, 1993.

2. Haunted Hooks (5.10d, 60 feet, sport) Found 15 feet right of Purple Haze, this line starts at the smaller of two left-leaning arches. 9 bolts. **FA:** Don Burroughs and Alan Busby, 1993.

3. Roto-Hammer (5.10c, 50 feet, sport) Just to the right of Haunted Hooks, this line starts at the large left-leaning arch. A stick clip is recommended, as several people have fallen—including this author—before clipping the first bolt. 7 bolts. **FA:** Daryl Ellis, 1992.

4. Nirvana (5.11a, 50 feet, sport) The fourth route from the left starts below a left-facing flake. A stick clip may be warranted for the second bolt if this line is at your limit. 7 bolts. **FA:** Don Burroughs and Alan Busby, 1993.

5. Stonehenge (5.11b, 50 feet, sport) Start in the deep hueco, right of Nirvana. Be careful at the second clip. 8 bolts. **FA:** Don Burroughs, Alan Busby, and Mike Ward, 1993.

6. Stone Hammer II (5.10d, 55 feet, mixed) This line—found right of Stonehenge—starts in an obvious crack. Send the crack and then blast out onto the face above the crack, passing three bolts to the anchor. At the time of this writing, at least one of the bolts needed replacement. Gear to 2 inches. **FA:** Mike Ward and Mike Clifford, 1986.

Stone Wall

PHOTO BY ANDY STEPHEN

7. Birthstone (5.10d, 55 feet, sport) This is the second to last line on the wall. Start at the right-facing flake and climb up to a shared anchor with Stone Hammer II. 6 bolts. **FA:** Leo and Karin Henson, 1993.

8. April Fools (5.10b, 50 feet, sport) The final route on the wall requires awkward movement up through a weird dish. It's best to pass this on the left and then continue up to the anchors. 6 bolts. **FA:** Don Burroughs and Alan Busby, 1993.

THE GALLERY

The Gallery is a very cool and very popular area. It harbors a handful of the most sought-after testpiece sport climbs in the conservation area, including routes like Yaak Crack and The Gift.

Several years ago I was directly below The Gallery when a Euro climber lowered off Yaak Crack. A super-psyched, super-young climber shouted, "That looked awesome! Was it good?"

The Euro responded with a smirk and a thick accent as he lowered: "For you, zis is good climb. But for me, maybe I do zis climb when I am sick or tired. But for you zis is good climb."

The Gallery

PHOTO BY DOUG FOUST

If people had been drinking beer, it would have blown out their noses. I don't think I've ever seen a group of people at a crag laugh so hard . . . and I've been repeating the story ever since!

Approach: From the Second Pull-Out, drop down the trail to the fork and go left. Hike up over a small outcrop and then drop down into the wash near a pine tree. Cross the wash and follow slabs up the hill to the crag. As you near the crag, it's possible to scramble up to the right-hand end of the wall, or more easily walk up to the left. **Time:** 20 minutes.

Sun Exposure: The Gallery is exposed to sun in the late morning and then is sunny the rest of the day.

Types of Climbing Available: Moderate to hard sport climbing, face climbing, and pumpy climbing

1. Range of Motion (5.10d, 40 feet, sport) This is the farthest line to the left before going around the corner to the next wall. While rated 5.10d, the crux is short. 4 bolts. **FA:** Todd Swain, Dick Peterson, and Peggy Bucky, 1990.

2. Trad Climbing Is Both (5.6, II, 250 feet, trad) The next bolted route is approximately 60 feet to the right of Range of Motion. This traditional line is in between the bolted routes and starts at an obvious right-leaning crack. **Pitch 1:** Climb up the crack for approximately 100 feet to a platform (5.6). **Pitch 2:** Climb up the face,

working up and left to a crack. Continue up to a platform with a rock pinched down by a giant boulder (5.6, 150 feet). **Descent:** Drop down the gully behind the climb to the right.

3. That Goode Dude Climb (5.7, 45 feet, sport) This is the first bolted sport climb to the right of Range of Motion. 5 bolts. **FA:** Mike Bond and Mike Moore, 2015.

4. Sport Climbing Is Neither (5.8+, 30 feet, sport) The next route on the wall is a little stout for the grade, but lots of fun. 3 bolts. **FA:** Unknown, 1991.

5. Buck's Muscle World (5.9, 30 feet, sport) The third route right of Trad Climbing Is Both is another short, mildly pumpy climb for the grade. 3 bolts. **FA:** Greg Mayer, 1990.

6. Gelatin Pooch (5.10a, 35 feet, sport) Found just right of Buck's Muscle World, this line climbs past four bolts to an anchor. 4 bolts. **FA:** Greg Mayer, 1990.

7. Pump First, Pay Later (5.10b, 40 feet, sport) As you continue along this wall, each route gets a little steeper. 4 bolts. **FA:** Greg Mayer, 1990.

8. Running Amuck (5.10c, 45 feet, sport) Found right of Pump First, this line starts at the base of a short, left-facing flake. 4 bolts. **FA:** Greg Mayer, 1990.

9. Gridlock (5.11a, 50 feet, sport) Right of Running Amuck, mantle up to clip the first bolt and then work right. Be sure to clip the third bolt from the crimps and climb to the jug after it's been clipped, to avoid a potentially nasty fall. Variation: For a 5.11c variation, start on Social Disorder and traverse up and left into Gridlock. 5 bolts. **FA:** Greg Mayer, 1990.

10. Social Disorder (5.11d, 50 feet, sport) Start up on the left side of a small black pod. Work up small edges to the right. Moving left takes you onto Gridlock. 5 bolts. **FA:** Scott Carson, Steve Bullock, and Jonathan Knight, 1991.

11. A Day in the Life (5.11c, 50 feet, sport) Start on the right side of the black-varnished pod and pull through crimps to the double-bolt anchor. **FA:** Bill Boyle, 1989.

12. Minstrel in the Gallery (5.12b, 55 feet, sport) This was the first route on the cliff. Send the line immediately right of A Day in the Life. A thin start leads to mildly easier but steeply overhung climbing above. It is possible to make the route a hair easier if you step across. 5 bolts. **FA:** Mike Tupper, 1989.

13. Yaak Crack (5.11c, 50 feet, sport) This super-popular line climbs up beside a left-leaning crack, but it is

The Gallery

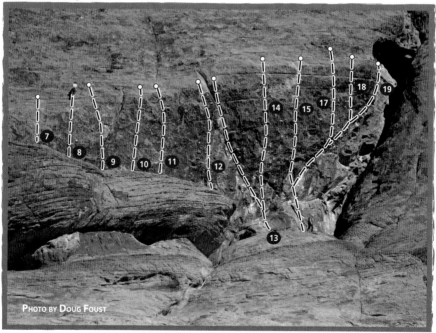

PHOTO BY DOUG FOUST

certainly not a crack climb. The line is steep, but the holds are big for the grade, though people often flame out near the top. 6 bolts. **FA:** Mike Tupper, 1989.

14. The Gift (5.12d, 55 feet, sport) This is one of the most famous routes of the grade in the country. Start as for Yaak Crack and blast straight up the line, climbing from easier 5.12a-type moves to a cruxy finish. 6 bolts—often rigged with fixed draws. **FA:** Boone Speed, 1989.

15. Sissy Traverse (5.13b, 90 feet, sport) One of the hardest pitches in Red Rock, the line starts up the first three bolts of The Gift and then traverses the wall to finish on Nothing Shocking. As this line requires bolts from multiple lines, it is seldom done. 9 bolts. **FA:** Don Welsh, 1991.

16. Where the Down Boys Go (5.12d, 55 feet, sport) Start 5 feet right of The Gift. 5 bolts. **FA:** Mick Tupper, 1989.

17. Who Made Who (5.12d, 55 feet, sport) This line shares a common start with Nothing Shocking and The Glitch. Start up as per The Glitch and then move up and right. 5 bolts. **FA:** Mike Tupper, 1990.

18. Nothing Shocking (5.13a, 60 feet, sport) Start as per The Glitch and then climb straight up. 6 bolts. **FA:** Don Welsh, 1989.

19. The Glitch (5.12c, 60 feet, sport) Climb up a right-leaning flake to a rest at a hueco. Power up the final moves to the anchor. 6 bolts. **FA:** Mike Tupper, 1990.

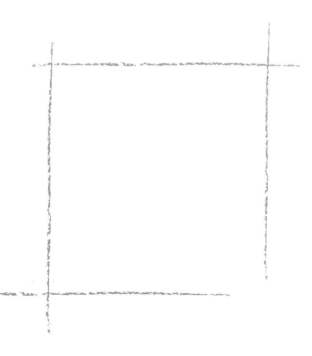

Sandstone Quarry

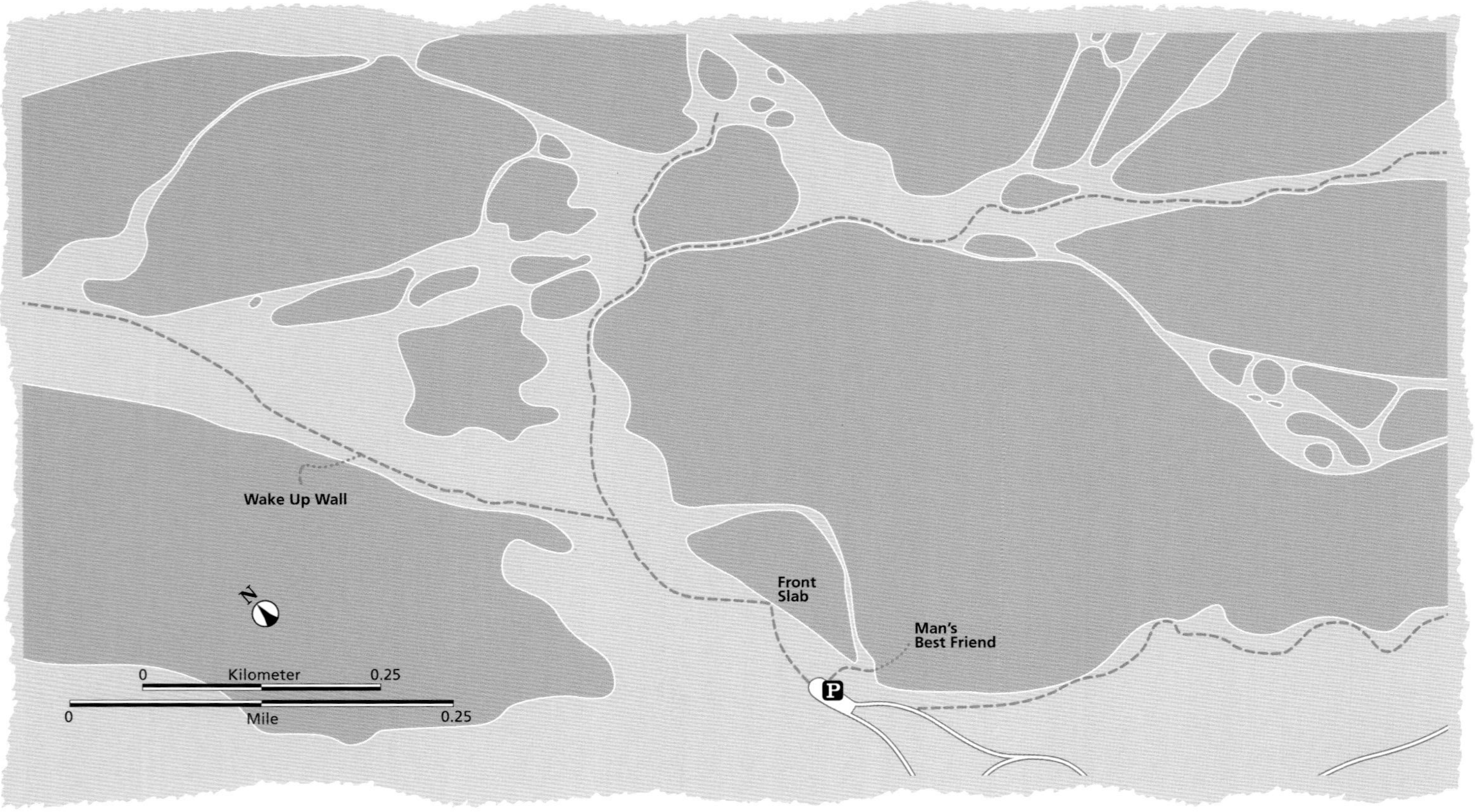

Front
Slab

Man's
Best Friend

P

Wake Up Wall

N

Kilometer

Mile

0   0.25

0   0.25

4.

Sandstone Quarry

In the early 1900s a company developed a small sandstone mining operation at what is now called the Sandstone Quarry. The operation provided sandstone to places like Las Vegas, Los Angeles, and San Francisco. But ultimately the operation was not profitable and had to close. The remnants of that early mine are seen throughout the area.

Today the Quarry is an incredibly popular tourist destination. First, it is arguably one of the friendliest pull-outs for those who visit Red Rock Canyon via bus. Second, it's an extremely popular trailhead, which means it caters to visitors with trekking poles. And third, there is climbing here. Some of the climbing is very close to the road, which also means it's a very good place for visitors to take pictures of posing climbers. Expect to become a part of someone's "My Trip to Vegas" slide show.

Approach: Enter the Red Rock Canyon Scenic Drive and drive 2.7 miles to the third pullout. Pull into the parking lot and park. Avoid parking off the road in the desert, and be sure not to block anybody in. Expect buses in this lot and park accordingly.

FRONT SLAB

When you park at the Sandstone Quarry, the Front Slab is literally right there! It is a mere 50 feet from the car and is easily identified by the large, arching, west-facing crack known as Fender Bender.

Approach: Take one of the braided trails to the base of the wall. All the routes on the Front Slab proper may be toproped. However, to do so you will have to walk to the left end of the crag and scramble up low-angled slabs before contouring back to the top of the crag. This will take about 15 minutes.

Sun Exposure: This wall migrates into the sun late in the morning and then remains exposed to the sun for the remainder of the day.

Types of Climbing Available:
Traditional crack climbing, slab climbing, sport, toprope, and one sport multi-pitch climb

1. Fender Bender (5.6, 50 feet, trad, TR) Climb up a short slab into the crack. Continue up the widening crack to the top. Pro to 3 inches. **FA:** Matt McMackin and Jim Whitesell, 1973.

2. Bent Bumper (5.8, 50 feet, TR) This line climbs directly up to the Fender Bender anchors. **FA:** Unknown.

3. Broken Taillight (5.8, 50 feet, TR) Climb the extremely slabby face immediately right of Bent Bumper. **FA:** Unknown.

Front Slab

4. Flat Tire (5.8, 50 feet, TR) Another slabby climb found to the right of Broken Taillight. Use the anchors for White Slab to toprope this climb. **FA:** Unknown.

5. White Slab (5.8, 50 feet, mixed) Send the bolted line 50 feet right of Fender Bender. Small gear will make this climb feel less exposed. Pro to 2 inches. **FA:** Unknown.

6. Man's Best Friend (5.7, 200 feet, sport) This route isn't actually on the Front Slab, but is instead found behind it. This wall (the Winston Wall) is south of the parking lot and easily identified by the tan rock that has a well-defined line where it changes to red. Depart from the south end of the parking lot and walk up low-angled slabs with a 3rd-class move here and there. Once on top of the slabs, look across a small gully to spot the anchors for the first pitch. Descend into the gully. Expect 4th-class moves with a 5th-class move at the bottom of the descent. There is a hueco thread-through that can be used to rappel if desired. **Pitch 1:** Climb up the obvious bolted line to a bolted anchor. The hardest move is at the first bolt, but it can be avoided by climbing slightly right (5.6–5.8, 100 feet). **Pitch 2:** Continue up the bolted line to the anchor (5.7, 100 feet). **Descent:** Make two single-rope rappels or one double-rope rappel.

Front Slab

WAKE UP WALL

Back in the day, people fought about this crag and the number of bolts on it. These battles have long faded, and today people are just psyched to climb at this cool little area!

Approach: Follow the main trail from the parking lot until it drops into the wash. Continue past a white boulder until you see a sign for Turtlehead Peak. Turn left on the trail and continue for 5 minutes until you climb up a dirt hump. From the top of the hump, several white crags are visible to the left (west). Continue on the trail on top of the hump until you reach some white rocks. The trail drops down into the wash, but don't follow it any farther. Instead, go left across the white slabs toward the north-facing Wake Up Wall. The crag faces Turtlehead Peak. The routes here are listed from left to right. **Time:** 15 minutes.

Sun Exposure: Very early morning sun and then shade the rest of the day.

Types of Climbing Available: Moderate to hard, steep sport climbing, with a few trad routes

1. Left Crack (5.10b, 60 feet, trad) This line on the far left side of the wall wanders up a crack to ring anchors. **FA:** Unknown.

2. The Last in Line (5.10b, 45 feet, sport) This first sport line on the far left-hand side of the wall is a tribute

Wake Up Wall

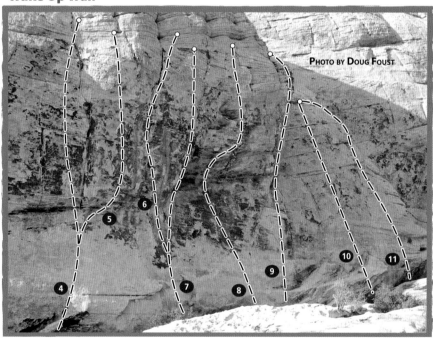

PHOTO BY DOUG FOUST

to the late Ronnie James Dio, the heavy-metal musician that popularized the devil fingers sign. It is recommended that you make this sign at the top of the route before lowering. The line starts in a small trough on patina. 6 bolts. **FA:** Mike Moore and Josh Gale, 2015.

3. Last Out (5.10a, 60 feet, mixed) The third route from the left blasts up past two bolts and into a crack system. Pro: Double up on 0.4 to 0.75 inch. **FA:** Unknown.

4. First Born (5.10b, 60 feet, sport) Originally put up as a mixed climb, this line climbs up through a small roof into a crack system. The crux is below the first bolt, and a stick clip is recommended. 6 bolts. **FA:** Ed Prochaska, 1990.

5. On to the Next One (5.11a, 50 feet, sport) Start as for First Born, but work up a right-trending rail. Continue up past a slab, a small roof, and a short runout to the top. Consider a stick clip for the second bolt. 7 bolts. **FA:** Mike Bond, Jenny Bond, and Mike Moore, 2011.

6. Spanky Spangler (5.10c, 50 feet, mixed) This line shares its start with Angled Dangler on the left side of a deep depression approximately a third of the way up the cliff. Make a bouldery start and then blast up left, eventually working back right to the anchor for Angled Dangler. 5 bolts, wires, and small cams. **FA:** Richard Harrison and Michelle Locatelli, 2007.

7. Angled Dangler (5.11d, 60 feet, sport) Start as for Spanky Spangler. Make the mantle move and then continue through the slab to the large overhang. The crux appears around the fifth bolt as the holds decrease in size. 6 bolts. **FA:** Richard Harrison and Michelle Locatelli, 2007.

8. Just Shut Up and Climb (5.11b, 60 feet, sport) Found to the right of Angled Dangler, this line starts on the right-hand side of the depression in the cliff. The line is mildly runout to the first bolt, and a stick clip is recommended. 5 bolts. **FA:** Randy Faulk and Dick Denison, 1991.

9. Mic's Master (5.10b, 55 feet, sport) Found immediately right of Just Shut Up and Climb. This line climbs the rib above the slab and is often considered a one-move-wonder-style route. Such a characterization is a bit of a fib. There are several harder moves, but it is not as sustained as the preceding lines. 5 bolts. **FA:** Michelle Locatelli, 2007.

10. Poundcake (5.8, 40 feet, sport) This line is found to the right of Mic's Master behind some scrub oak. 3 bolts. **FA:** Jay and Gail Meuller, 1997.

11. Crack of Noon (5.8 R, 40 feet, trad) Follow some thin cracks to the right of Poundcake. The line shares an anchor with that route. Pro: Stoppers, small cams. **FA:** Jay and Gail Meuller, 1997.

12. Too Few Years (5.11a, 50 feet, sport) Found just right of Poundcake and Crack of Noon, this line climbs up the face, linking thin seams. 5 bolts. **FA:** Mike Bond, Malcolm Babbitt, and Marc Dudas, 2011.

13. The Shape of Things to Come (5.11a, 35 feet, sport) Found right of Too Few Years, this route climbs up past three glue-in bolts to an anchor. 3 bolts. **FA:** Greg Mayer, 1989.

14. The Healer (5.11d, 35 feet, sport) Found approximately 5 feet right of The Shape of Things to Come, this route works up from a techy start to a seam. Follow thin moves to the fourth bolt, where the climbing becomes easier. 4 bolts. **FA:** Greg Mayer, 1990.

15. Rise and Whine (5.12a, 35 feet, sport) Found just right of The Healer, this line shares its anchor with that route. 4 bolts. **FA:** Mike Tupper, 1990.

16. Pain Check (5.12a, 40 feet, sport) This line shares an anchor with Good Mourning. Thin climbing gets thinner with a crux at the fourth bolt. 4 bolts. **FA:** Bill Boyle, 1990.

17. Good Mourning (5.11b, 40 feet, sport) The next line on the wall starts just left of a small seam. This line shares an anchor with Pain Check. 5 bolts. **FA:** Bill Boyle, 1990.

18. Native Son (5.11c, 40 feet, sport) This line starts on the left-hand side of the hueco right of Good Mourning. 5 bolts. **FA:** Mike Tupper, 1990.

19. Where Egos Dare (5.12a, 40 feet, sport) This line starts in the hueco just right of Native Son. The route is found left of the chimney and arête feature. Climb up through the hueco on crimps to easier—but not that much easier—climbing above. 4 bolts. **FA:** Greg Mayer, 1991.

20. XTZ (5.8, 30 feet, sport) The next route to the right follows a line up a deep cleft/offwidth. There are three bolts on this short line. Some may wish to use gear as well, but it is not required for a reasonably safe ascent. **FA:** Greg Mayer, spring 1990.

21. Onsight Flight (5.12b, 40 feet, sport) This line starts just right of the chimney/offwidth and follows sustained sloping crimpers up a slightly overhanging feature of the wall. **FA:** Don Welsh, 1990.

Wake Up Wall

PHOTO BY DOUG FOUST

20 is in the left leaning chimney. Routes 23-27 are in the box on the right.

22. Stand and Deliver (5.12c, 40 feet, sport) The second route to the right of the chimney/offwidth is another hard sporty route. 4 bolts. **FA:** Mike Tupper, 1990.

23. The Last Drag (5.9+, 50 feet, sport) Found to the right of Stand and Deliver. 5 bolts. **FA:** Mike Bond, 2011.

24. Blame It on My ADD (5.9, 50 feet, sport) Found 10 feet right of The Last Drag. Climb past five bolts to a mussy hook anchor. **FA:** Mike Bond, 2011.

25. Fall of Vegas (5.10a, 50 feet, sport) Found 10 feet right of Blame It on My ADD. Climb through a cruxy start to easier 5.9ish climbing above. **FA:** Mike Bond, 2011.

26. Skid Mark (5.10a, 50 feet, sport) This line on the right-hand side of the wall makes its way up a black streak. 7 bolts. **FA:** Travis Graves and Phillip Swiny, 2007.

27. The Big Short (5.8, 50 feet, sport) The final route on the wall is found 10 feet right of Skid Mark in a gully. 4 bolts. **FA:** Mike Bond, 2011.

Angel Food Wall

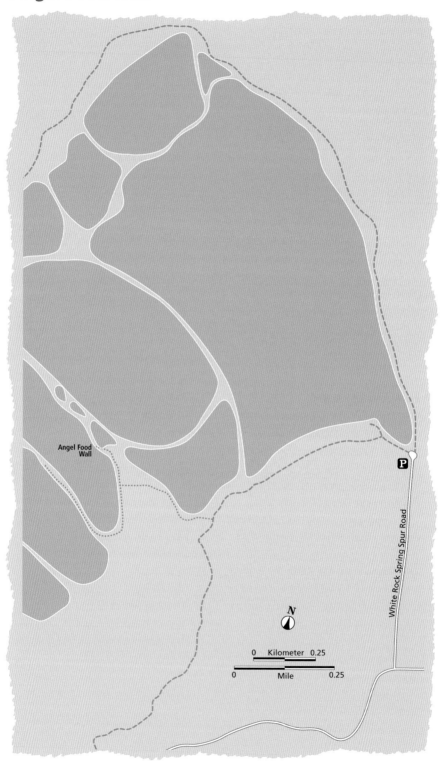

Angel Food
Wall

White Rock Spring Spur Road

N

0   Kilometer   0.25

0   Mile   0.25

5.

Angel Food Wall

The Angel Food Wall is an absolutely beautiful piece of sandstone on White Rock Peak. The wall is grooved with several deep crack and chimney systems, which provide some of the most popular moderate lines in the area.

In the early 1970s the Angel Food Wall became one of the go-to places for a small but developing group of local climbers. Several new routes were put up during those years, but the most important was certainly Tunnel Vision. This route, which was climbed in 1974 by Joe Herbst and Randal Grandstaff, quickly became the first Red Rock mega-classic.

There are a dozen routes on the Angel Food Wall, but the three lines listed here are absolutely stellar. Due to the inevitable crowding, teams should prepare for all three routes and then climb whichever is least busy.

Approach: Follow the Red Rock Canyon Scenic Drive for 5.8 miles. Turn right on a gravel road and drive an additional 0.5 mile to a small parking area with an outhouse. The Angel Food Wall on White Rock Peak is clearly visible from the lot.

From the parking lot take the trail on an old abandoned road downhill (south). A couple of minutes from the lot, the trail forks. Take the left fork and continue down the old roadbed.

After approximately 10 minutes the trail is at its closest point to the wall.

Several braided trails cut away from the roadbed toward the wall; some of them are more obvious and better marked than others. As you cross the desert toward the wall, you'll notice a steep trail in red dirt that works its way up to the base: Aim for this.

Once at the top of the steep red dirt trail, look for a tree in red dirt on slightly angled terrain below the wall. All additional approaches start from this tree.

Sun Exposure: The bulk of Tunnel Vision doesn't see any sun at all. The rest of the wall gets morning sun. This is a good wall for a hot day.

Types of Climbing Available: Multi-pitch, moderate trad climbs, some chimney and offwidth

1. Tunnel Vision (5.7+ R, III, 700 feet, trad) An awesome route with a very cool pitch through the mountain high up. To be comfortable on this route, climbers should be solid 5.8 leaders, as there are some runouts on moderate terrain. This line primarily follows corners and a chimney system on the left side of the wall. To get to the base of the route, continue up from the tree and turn right on the trail. Scramble up a 6-foot step and make your way to the

Tunnel Vision

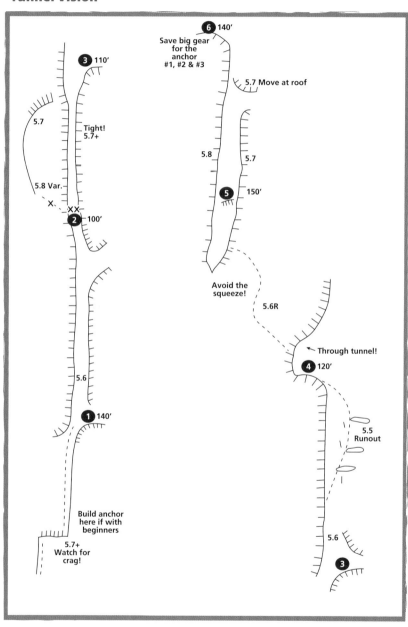

6 140'

Save big gear for the anchor #1, #2 & #3

5.7 Move at roof

3 110'

5.7

Tight! 5.7+

5.8

5.7

5.8 Var.

X.

XX

5 150'

2 100'

Avoid the squeeze!

5.6R

Through tunnel!

5.6

4 120'

1 140'

5.5 Runout

Build anchor here if with beginners

5.7+ Watch for crag!

5.6

3

base of the route below a small overhang. The overhang is approximately 10 feet up, and a crack works its way up to it and then traverses right below it. **Pitch 1:** Climb up the crack to the roof and the hand traverse. Traverse right and then pull through the roof. If you are with a beginner, you may want to belay as soon as possible after the roof, as communication is difficult higher. If you are a solid party, continue up the crack system and the face, pulling up on a small ledge. Continue past the ledge through a chimney to a second ledge. Belay below the wide chimney (5.7+, 140 feet). Variation: It is also possible to climb the bolted face to the right of the route at 5.9. **Pitch 2:** Continue up the chimney above. When you reach the slit where it is possible to go right or left, stay left into another chimney. Build a very uncomfortable anchor at the bolted belay station in the chimney (5.6, 100 feet). **Pitch 3:** There are two options here. It is possible to work out left, passing a couple of bolts and protecting the crack until the line arcs back in at the top of the chimney, or you can climb the chimney. The chimney is rated R, but is very cool. There is more gear if you arc out left. At the top of the chimney, continue up the crack system to a large ledge in a small alcove. Big pro may be desirable for the chimney variation (5.7+, 110 feet). **Pitch 4:** Climb up out of the alcove onto the face. It's possible to stay in the right-facing corner for a while, where there is a bit more pro, but you will eventually have to

work out onto the face where the pro is thinner. When the opportunity presents itself, climb back into the corner to finish the pitch. Build an anchor on the large ledge at the base of the cave pitch (5.6, 120 feet). **Pitch 5:** This is the infamous tunnel pitch. An old guidebook recommended a headlamp, but it's generally bright enough inside to see. There are two things to remember on this pitch. First, if you're squirming through a pinch, you're off-route and are probably too far left too early. And second, pay attention to the wall behind you for protection. From the ledge, walk back into the tunnel and climb up ripples in the smooth sandstone, working your way left as you go. Eventually you will come to a rail. Step up on the rail and walk left to exit the cave. Climb up the chimney system for another 20 feet to a good stance and build a belay (5.6 R, 150 feet). **Pitch 6:** Continue up the wide chimney (the right-hand side is a bit easier) to a small roof. Pull the roof and continue up the crack system to a ledge on the left (5.7, 140 feet). **Descent:** Scramble down the backside of the ledge to a short chimney. Drop down to the base of the chimney onto a massive rocking boulder and continue down the gully below. The gully will eventually end, and you will contour right on some mildly exposed slabs into a larger gully. If you go straight down from where you join the larger gully, you will have to make a rappel. Instead, scramble across the rib to an easier 3rd- and 4th-class descent. Make your way down

Angel Food Wall

PHOTO BY ANDY STEPHEN

Descent
Gully

1

2

3

the main gully system to the bottom of the mountain. Follow braided trails skier's left around the base of the feature and back to the bottom of the route. Pro to 4 inches. **FA:** Joe Herbst and Randal Grandstaff, 1974.

2. Group Therapy (5.7, III, 800 feet, trad) This route—just right of Tunnel Vision—is defined by the crack system capped by a massive roof. The route climbs an awesome chimney to the right of that roof. From the tree, work up toward the base of Tunnel Vision, but instead of climbing the small step, continue working right on the brushy trail. Follow the trail until you are at the base of a large chimney. Before entering the chimney, you will find a block

beneath cracks and a honeycombed face. Rack up here. **Pitch 1:** Climb up cracks and honeycombed rock to a stance below a nice-looking vertical crack. There are some thread-throughs here in the honeycombed rock that can be used to help build your anchor (5.6, 140 feet). **Pitch 2:** Continue up into the crack system above. Note that the crack will get quite wide, so be sure to place gear where possible. Continue up to a stance at a horizontal crack system (5.6, 80 feet). **Pitch 3:** Work up the crack system to another small stance at a tree. It is possible to split this pitch into two pitches if needed for communication (5.5, 180 feet). Variation: From the top of pitch 3, it is possible to work left, placing pro where possible and diagonaling up to the bottom of the tunnel pitch of Tunnel Vision (5.6, 150 feet). The climbing on Group Therapy is much easier to this point than on Tunnel Vision, and this may be an option for a strong, fast team that wishes to pass slower Tunnel Vision parties and climb the tunnel pitch. **Pitch 4:** Climb up to the base of the chimney and build a semi-hanging belay (5.5, 75 feet). **Pitch 5:** Blast up the chimney. Be sure to place pro whenever possible, as it is mildly runout. Most people have to do several pirouettes in the chimney. Eventually you will reach a large ledge on the right. Build an anchor here. Large pro is desirable on this pitch (5.7, 100 feet). **Pitch 6:** There are two options to finish out the route. You can climb out of the crack system on the left to escape (5.4, 100 feet). Or you can work straight up through a short offwidth and a roof (5.8, 110 feet). **Descent:** Scramble down climber's left to join the descent for Tunnel Vision. Pro to 4 inches. Many people will want double #4s and maybe a #5. If you don't have double #4s, this route is rated R. **FA:** Joe and Betsy Herbst, Randal Grandstaff, and Matt McMackin, 1974.

3. Purblind Pillar (5.8, III, 900 feet, trad) The newest addition to the Angel Food Wall is in an incredibly cool position, and also happens to be the longest line on the wall. From the tree, climb up toward the base of Tunnel Vision, but do not scramble up to the base. Continue on the brushy trail right of Tunnel Vision to a deep gully/chimney. Continue past that and scramble up through brush to a giant corner. The line climbs a crack system to the left of a large buttress. **Pitch 1:** Climb the left-facing corner system and crack, passing a little vegetation down low. Continue up to a small stance on this rope-stretcher of a pitch (5.7, 190 feet). **Pitch 2:** Traverse right, following a crack to a bolt and a 5.8 move. The climb eases as you climb below another crack system to a small ledge (5.8, 75 feet). **Pitch 3:** Traverse right for approximately 20 feet. Climb up into the gully above, working up cracks for 30 feet to a bolt. Traverse into another crack system until you reach a large ledge below yet another crack system (5.7, 150 feet). **Pitch 4:** Climb up the crack system above until it ends. From there, work out left on a ledge system above a brush-choked gully to a double-bolt anchor (5.7, 180 feet). **Pitch 5:** Climb up off the ledge, passing a bolt and into small cracks. Continue up easier ground until you can traverse onto a ledge below a large left-facing dihedral (5.8, 120 feet). **Pitch 6:** Climb up to the base of the large dihedral. Scrub oak blocks the entrance to an ugly-looking offwidth. Don't climb up into the offwidth; instead climb left just below it and clip a bolt. Continue up, passing another bolt, then back into the crack system to the top (5.7, 195 feet). **Descent:** Scramble down the brushy gully climber's left to join the Tunnel Vision descent. Pro to 4 inches.

Willow Springs

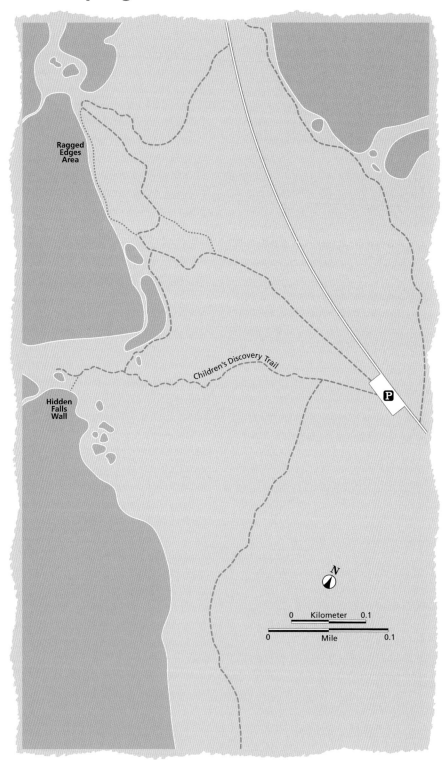

Ragged
Edges
Area

Children's Discovery Trail

Hidden
Falls
Wall

P

N

0   Kilometer   0.1

0   Mile   0.1

6.

Willow Springs

The Willow Springs area is home to a great number of pleasant single-pitch traditional climbs. The area is also home to a picnic area, some child-friendly trails, and several petroglyphs. Like the Sandstone Quarry and the First Pullout, you should expect to have a lot of tourists gawking while you climb here. Unfortunately, litter and noise pollution tend to come with them, but so too do the occasional bikini and beefcake photo shoots. As such, sometimes it can be a bit difficult to concentrate on climbing . . . welcome to Las Vegas!

It should go without saying that climbing on petroglyphs is a serious faux pas. Indeed, nothing threatens access more. So please, do not climb on the petroglyphs.

Approach: To get to Willow Springs, enter the Red Rock Canyon Scenic Drive and go 7.3 miles to a paved road that cuts off to the right. Park in any of the small lots scattered throughout the area.

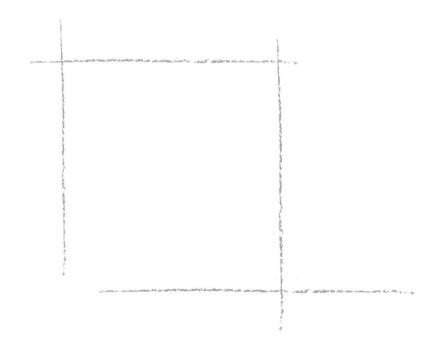

HIDDEN FALLS WALL

This is a super-fun little gem of a wall near the back of the Hidden Falls Canyon. There have been a few spats about bolts in this area, which is too bad. No matter what you read on the Internet, all the routes in the area are—or were—enjoyable.

Approach: The spur road from the scenic drive has two parking areas on the south side of the road. The first parking area is where the Children's Discovery Trail starts. Follow this trail to a wooden boardwalk. Shortly after the end of the boardwalk, a pair of boulders will appear on the right side of the trail. Leave the main trail here and walk left of the boulders. The Hidden Falls Wall is just beyond. **Time:** 15 minutes.

Sun Exposure: This wall is in the shade all day.

Types of Climbing Available: Steep crack and face climbing, some moderates and some harder lines, both trad and sport

1. Pointless and Stupid (5.8, 100 feet, sport—maybe) This line on the far left edge of the crag climbs up a small feature to a ledge and then continues up on the face above. The line has been stripped of bolts once or twice. As you read this, the route may or may not be there. **FA:** Unknown.

2. Killer Clowns (5.10c, 100 feet, trad) This slightly runout line is right of Pointless and Stupid and left of the Left Out crack. Work your way up a chimney to a thin crack. Continue up, passing a bolt to the top of the feature and an anchor. Pro to 3 inches—consider doubles of the 3-inch piece. **FA:** Paul Van Betten, Sal Mamusia, Richard Harrison, and Kevin Biernacki, 1989.

3. Left Out (5.10d, 90 feet, trad) Left Out is a testpiece trad climb: It's steep, fun, and pumpy! Blast up the arête to the obvious crack. Continue up the crack to the top of the feature. Some have complained that this route is runout. That is not the case. Keep your eyes open for good pro. Pro to 3 inches. Double up in the middle range. **FA:** Joe Herbst, 1975.

4. Outrageous Fortune (5.13b, 90 feet, sport) A very smooth bolted face is to the right of Left Out. Teeny tiny edges work up past bolts to an anchor. The first bolt is high, and a longish stick clip is recommended. 9 bolts.

5. Black Track (5.9, 100 feet, trad) This line climbs the spectacular right-leaning crack with a little bit of off-width found in the center of the wall. Pro to 4 inches. **FA:** Joe Herbst, 1973.

Hidden Falls Wall

6. Stupid Foot (5.11a, 90 feet, TR) String your rope down from Black Track and climb the face immediately right of it.

7. Big Foot (5.10a, 60 feet, sport) This line to the right of Stupid Foot is a bit runout for a Red Rock sport climb, but it is still a lot of fun. Climb up the ramp to honeycombed rock and crimpier climbing above. 4 bolts. **FA:** Mark Robinson, Eric Keto, and Al Rubin, 1989.

8. Camel Toe (5.10a, 60 feet, sport) This line climbs up the face to the right of Big Foot. 3 bolts. **FA:** Unknown.

9. Buffalo Balls (5.11d, 40 feet, sport) This short climb starts on top of the little buttress. The line is easier than the appointed grade if you use the crack. 4 bolts. **FA:** Bob Yoho, 1989, on TR; Don Burroughs and Alan Busby, 1992, for the lead.

RAGGED EDGES AREA

The Ragged Edges area is an awesome little area with several high-quality crack climbs. The crag is easily identified from the road by the beautiful Ragged Edges crack that splits the dark protruding cliff that is almost directly opposite the Willow Springs Picnic Area.

Approach: To get to this cliffband, park at one of the Willow Springs parking areas and take any of the trails that cut toward the cliff on the south of the road. Keep an eye on the route and follow the most logical trail toward it. A few minutes from the base of the cliff, leave the established trails and take one of the braided and brushy climber's trails to the base of the wall. **Time:** 10 minutes.

Sun Exposure: These routes receive morning sun and afternoon shade.

Types of Climbing Available: Moderate trad and mixed climbing, some crack and face

1. Go Ahead and Jump (5.6, 110 feet, trad) On the left side of the crag, a few feet right of a big white boulder leaning against the wall, a nice crack system shoots all the way to the large ledge approximately 100 feet up. This tends to be one of the driest routes to the left of Kemosabe. Many people break this short route into two pitches. The first pitch is recommended. The second pitch is a wide, ugly chimney and is not recommended. **Pitch 1:** Climb the crack and belay at a convenient tree just before the system widens. The tree makes for a good toprope anchor. There is an old bolt left of the crack about 40 feet up. While you might not trust this for pro, it makes for a good directional piece for toproping (5.6, 60 feet). **Pitch 2:** Wallow up the wide chimney for 50 more feet to a big ledge and a second tree (5.6, 50 feet). **Descent:** Walk climber's right along the easy 2nd- and 3rd-class ledge and make a 100-foot rappel down Tonto. Pro to 3 inches. **FA:** Joe Herbst, 1970s.

2. Dense Dunce (5.8 R, 70 feet, trad) This line is found just right of Go Ahead and Jump. Send the black varnished rock through huecos to a ledge three-quarters of the way up the wall. A trad anchor is required. **Descent:** Rappel from the first possible belay tree on Go Ahead and Jump to the left. Pro to 4 inches. **FA:** Wendell Broussard, 1984.

3. OK OK OK! (5.6+, 70 feet, trad) Send the crack to the right of Dense Dunce. This line is often wet after a storm. Rappel Go Ahead and Jump. Pro to 4 inches. **FA:** Joe Herbst, 1970s.

4. Kemosabe (5.10a R, 105 feet, trad) This awesome line climbs the outside edge of a huge arching corner. Climb the arête to a thin crack. As the crack peters out, continue up the face past a bolt to the top. Pro to 2 inches.

Ragged Edges Area

Small gear is good. **FA:** Sal Mamusia, Paul Van Betten, Nick Nordblom, Richard Harrison, Bob Conz, Pauline Schroeder, and Wendell Broussard, 1993.

5. Tonto (5.5, 100 feet, trad) This line is found immediately right of the giant arch of Kemosabe. Climb up the seam and work to the right before attaining the roof. Follow left-facing corners to the top. Pro to 3 inches. **FA:** Joe and Betsy Herbst, 1972.

6. The Lone Ranger (5.9, 100 feet, trad or TR) Climb the varnished face to the right of Tonto. This line can be toproped after leading Tonto. **FA:** Unknown.

7. Theme Book (5.9 R, 110 feet, trad) Just to the right of The Lone Ranger, there is a large left-facing corner and chimney system that works its way to the top of the crag. This is a good route for 5.9 offwidth practice; as such, you should bring offwidth protection. **FA:** Joe Herbst, 1973.

8. Vision Quest (5.12d, 160 feet, mixed) This is the line that climbs the left edge of the main wall, right of Theme Book. It is sometimes broken into two pitches. Pro to 2.5 inches. **FA:** Paul Van Betten and Sal Mamusia, 1988.

9. Bodiddly (5.11a R, 180 feet, mixed) This line climbs the steep face to the right of Vision Quest. The rock is a bit friable. Start on the arête and then launch up and right, passing three bolts. Continue up over a steep bulge to easier climbing above. Pro to 3 inches; mid-range doubles and micro-nuts may be desired. **FA:** Richard Harrison and Robert Finlay, 1985.

10. Plan F (5.10a or 5.11a, 60 or 180 feet, trad) Immediately left of the deep and obvious crack system in the main wall, locate a thinner, right-angling crack that works its way up to a double-bolt anchor. The first pitch of this crack is 5.10a, and the second pitch is 5.11a. Many parties only climb the first pitch, or toprope that pitch from the Ragged Edges anchor. Pro to 3 inches, with lots of small gear. Micro-nuts may be desired for the second pitch. **FA:** Sal Mamusia, Richard Harrison, Paul Van Betten, and Nick Nordblom, 1983.

11. Ragged Edges (5.8, 190 feet, trad) This is the beautiful crack that splits the center of the main face. The line can be done as one long pitch or as a two-pitch endeavor. Many people only climb the first pitch, as the second pitch is wide and mildly runout. If you do climb the second pitch, walk off to the right or scramble over to the top of Tonto on the left and make a 100-foot rappel. Pro: **Pitch 1:** to 3 inches; **Pitch 2:** doubles to 4 inches. **FA:** Joe Herbst and Jeff Lansing, 1970.

12. Chicken Eruptus (5.10b R, 200 feet, trad) Found just right of Ragged Edges, this old-school line climbs up a right-trending ramp to a bolt. Continue up the path of least resistance, passing another bolt on the way. Many people find this line to be bolder than other routes of its grade in the conservation area. It is possible to escape right approximately halfway up. Pro to 3 inches, with lots of small gear. **FA:** Richard Harrison, Wendell Broussard, Paul Van Betten, and Sal Mamusia, 1983.

13. Akido Gun Boy (5.11d R, 90 feet, mixed) This line, found 15 feet to the right of Chicken Eruptus, is what is often referred to as a "big boy underpants" climb. It is a bold route. Work up through a bouldery start to the first bolt. Continue up, staying left of a black streak and passing two more bolts to the top. As you approach a ledge, traverse out right to attain it and to finish the climb. Because you are on hard 5.11 terrain with marginal gear below, clipping the second bolt is super scary. It is possible to climb the first half of Chicken Eruptus to the escape to set up a toprope for this climb. To descend, walk off right from the terrace mid-face. Pro to 2 inches, including micro-nuts. **FA:** Paul Van Betten, Richard Harrison, Sal Mamusia, and Danny Meyers, 1991.

14. Sheep Trail (5.10b R, 90 feet, trad) Another bold route is found just right of Akido Gun Boy. There are several possible starts to the line, and some are easier than others. Start by bouldering up through white rock on the right. The route cuts back and forth a few times as you follow the line of least resistance into a shallow, left-facing corner system. Descend from the terrace halfway up the crag by walking right. Pro to 3 inches. **FA:** John Bachar, Mike Lechlinski, and Richard Harrison, 1983.

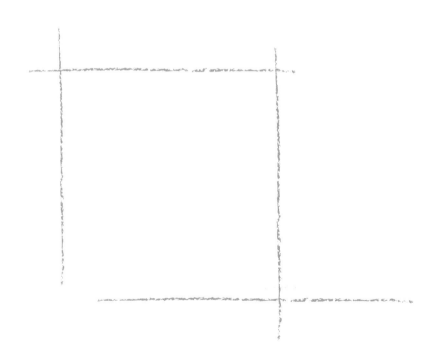

A climber works through a variation from the pitch 4 belay on Frigid Air Buttress. Photo by Jared Drapala

7.

Icebox Canyon

Icebox Canyon is a beautiful place. Spectacular buttresses and walls of clean sandstone shoot up on either side of you. There are several seasonal waterfalls. And indeed, when it's very cold occasionally large waterfall ice formations appear; amazingly enough, some of these have even been climbed. As such, it can certainly be cold here, especially in the winter, which makes sense—the place is referred to as Icebox Canyon.

As with many other areas in the conservation area, parking is tight at the trailhead. This shouldn't be a problem for early risers, but on a sunny spring day, it can be a serious issue by late morning.

Approach: Follow the Red Rock Canyon Scenic Drive for 7.8 miles to the parking area at the trailhead.

Icebox Canyon

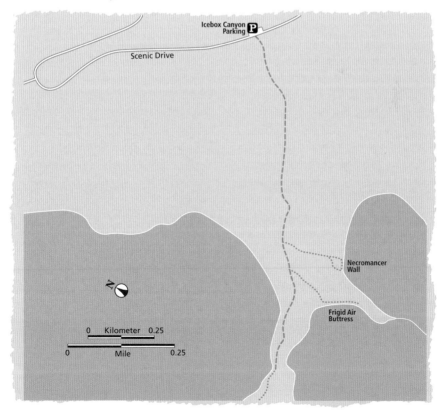

FRIGID AIR BUTTRESS

In many ways the Frigid Air Buttress is an absolutely beautiful piece of rock. Indeed, the line by the same name that weaves its way up the buttress is one of the most classic of its grade in the conservation area. And while the route is utterly fantastic, it should be noted that the buttress was also the scene of an early Red Rock tragedy.

In 1980 Betsy Herbst—wife of the prolific Red Rock pioneer, Joe Herbst—was leading a friend up the Frigid Air Buttress when something went wrong. The young woman tied herself off and went limp.

Joe Herbst and Randal Grandstaff had just finished a nearby route and were hanging out on the ground when they noted that there was a problem near the top of the buttress. The pair sprang into action, climbing as fast as they could until they reached Betsy. But there was nothing they could do. She wasn't injured, and there was no visible trauma to repair. Instead, she had suffered a stroke.

The team was able to evacuate Betsy from the climb and get her to a hospital, but unfortunately it was too late. The young climber passed away a short time later.

The tragedy was threefold. Joe lost his beloved wife, the community lost a wonderful friend, and Red Rock Canyon lost Joe. After Betsy died, his passion for the sport withered, and he never made another major ascent.

Approach: Park at the trail-head for Icebox Canyon and hike for approximately 15 minutes. Cut off to the left, following intermittent trails through the wash and then through boulders to the base of the buttress. Frigid Air Buttress starts behind a large boulder, just left of the prow's center. **Time:** 25 minutes.

Sun Exposure: The feature sees morning sun in the warmer months. As the sun gets lower in the sky, the amount of sun the route receives diminishes.

Types of Climbing Available: A long, varied trad climb with crack and offwidth climbing, followed by a complex descent

1. Frigid Air Buttress (5.9+, IV-, 900 feet, trad) **Pitch 1:** Follow the flake and crack, passing a bolted anchor. Continue up a crack, working left into a gully. Climb up a short slab to a tree (5.7, 190 feet). **Pitch 2:** Continue up cracks in the wall above to a bushy ledge. Move right on the ledge into a corner. Climb up and left to another large ledge (5.8, 160 feet). **Pitch 3:** Work up the chimney until you can step left onto the easy face that terminates at another ledge (5.4, 100 feet). **Pitch 4:** Work up the widening crack above to a break in the crack system and a bolt. Continue up through the offwidth section (5.8ish) to another ledge, approximately 20 feet beyond the offwidth. It's possible to avoid

Frigid Air Buttress

PHOTO BY ANDY STEPHEN

Frigid Air Buttress

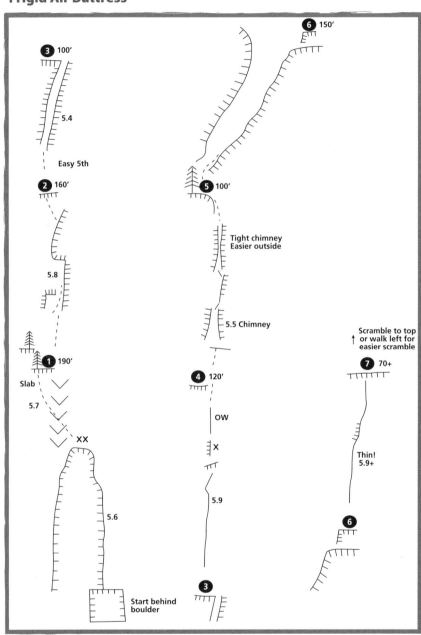

3 100'

5.4

Easy 5th

2 160'

5.8

Slab

1 190'

5.7

XX

5.6

Start behind
boulder

6 150'

5 100'

Tight chimney
Easier outside

5.5 Chimney

4 120'

OW

X

5.9

3

Scramble to top
↑ or walk left for
easier scramble

7 70+

Thin!
5.9+

6

the offwidth by climbing a 5.4 ramp up and right (5.9, 120 feet). **Pitch 5:** Work up a short but wide chimney to a leftward hand traverse. Continue up to a narrow chimney. Stem up outside the chimney, working your way up to a large ledge on the left. Belay at the pine tree in the corner (5.9, 100 feet). **Pitch 6:** Climb up the inside corner behind the tree. Continue up easy huecos to a belay behind the final headwall and the steep-looking crack above (5.6, 150 feet). **Pitch 7:** Climb the beautiful varnished crack to a large ledge (5.9+, 70 feet). **Pitch 8:** Scramble up the final short wall, or walk around to the left and complete an easier scramble to the top (5.0, 100 feet). **Descent:** Drop down the gully climber's left to a series of chockstones, and note that there is a chimney hidden beneath them. Either rappel or downclimb the chimney to a flat area below. A ramp drops down from here toward The Maze, a popular canyoneering route. Don't follow the ramp down, instead work south, following cairns to a pine tree approximately 60 feet uphill of The Maze. Make a 60-foot rappel to a big ledge. Make a second 190-foot rappel to a bolted rap station. Make a third 100-foot rappel to a big ledge and then make a final 100-foot rappel to the base of the wall. Bring double ropes for the descent and pro to 4 inches. **FA:** Joe Herbst and Larry Hamilton, March 1976.

NECROMANCER WALL

A necromancer is supposed to be able to communicate with the dead. Climbers can't do that. I know because they have a hard enough time communicating with the living. I hear proof in every canyon throughout Red Rock, every day. You hear them yell, "OFF BELAY!"

And then the climber's partner responds, "WHAT?"

"OFF BELAY!"

"WHAT? ARE YOU OFF . . .?"

"OFF BELAY!"

"I CAN'T HEAR YOU! I'M! TAKING! YOU! OFF! BELAY!"

"AM I STILL ON BELAY!"

"SORRY! I'LL PUT YOU BACK ON!"

So, from this we can assume that the darkly varnished, little triangular-shaped wall on the south side of the canyon was not named for a climber's skill at communication. And it certainly wasn't named for a climber's skill at communing with ghosts.

Approach: From the Icebox Canyon parking area, hike the main trail until you are almost directly across from the Necromancer Wall. Take one of the braided trails steeply down into the wash. Continue to follow braided trails to the base of the wall. **Time:** 25 minutes.

Sun Exposure: This north-facing wall is in the shade all day most of the year. It sees a short period of afternoon sun in the spring.

Types of Climbing Available: Single and multi-pitch trad crack and face climbing

Necromancer Wall

PHOTO BY ANDY STEPHEN

1. Hop Route (5.7+, I+, 275 feet, trad) This line is found just right of the large pillar leaning against the triangular wall. **Pitch 1:** Climb up the nice—albeit a bit funky—hand crack to the right of the right-facing corner. Follow the crack as it works into the corner and then belay on top of the pillar. Some choose to rappel from threaded slings here (5.7+, 100 feet). Variation: Climb straight up the right-facing corner, but bring big gear! You may want a 5-inch cam (5.7+, 100 feet). **Pitch 2:** Scramble up left on top of the pillar to a long crack. Follow this to the summit (5.6, 175 feet). **Descent:** Descend the gully climber's left. Three single-rope rappels or one double-rope rappel will take you to the base. Pro to 4 inches. **FA:** Joe Hop and Joe and Betsy Herbst, 1975.

2. Black Magic Panties (5.10a R, 110 feet, trad) This bold line is found just between the Hop Route and Sensuous Mortician. Climb up varnished rock, placing pro as it presents itself. As you get higher, the pro gets thinner. Clip two bolts below the roof and then climb through it just right of a crack. Belay above the roof. **Descent:** Traverse to the Hop Route or to Sensuous Mortician to continue up or descend. Pro to 3 inches, with extra small gear. **FA:** Nick Nordblom, Jenni Stone, and Danny Rider, 1988.

3. Sensuous Mortician (5.9, 120 feet, trad) An excellent single-pitch moderate. Start on the right side of a large block that hangs about 10 feet above the ground. Work up the crack as it arches slightly to the right until it peters out. Continue to follow the line of least resistance up the face and through a small roof to a belay. **Descent:** Either rappel the route with double ropes or continue up the second pitch of Fold Out. Pro to 3 inches. **FA:** Nick Nordblom and John Martinet, 1979.

4. Fold Out (5.8, 300 feet, trad) Approximately 25 feet right of Sensuous Mortician, on the far right-hand side of the Necromancer Wall, is an obvious crack system. **Pitch 1:** Climb up the obvious and relatively easy crack system. Approximately two-thirds of the way up the route, the juggy climbing goes away and there is a 15-foot section of 5.8ish crack climbing that is reminiscent of the last pitch on Birdland in Pine Creek Canyon. Belay at the double-bolt anchor (5.8, 130 feet). **Pitch 2:** Work up and left, aiming toward the water streak and groove above. Work through a short thin section and clip a bolt. Continue up a crack to a tree (5.8, 100 feet). **Pitch 3:** Climb up to the top of the feature, left of a chimney and crack system (5.4, 70 feet). **Descent:** Descend as for the Hop Route. Pro to 3 inches. **FA:** Tom Kaufman and Joe Herbst, 1976.

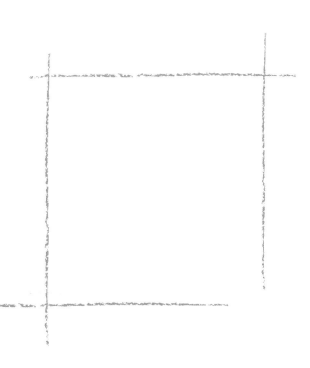

Pine Creek Canyon

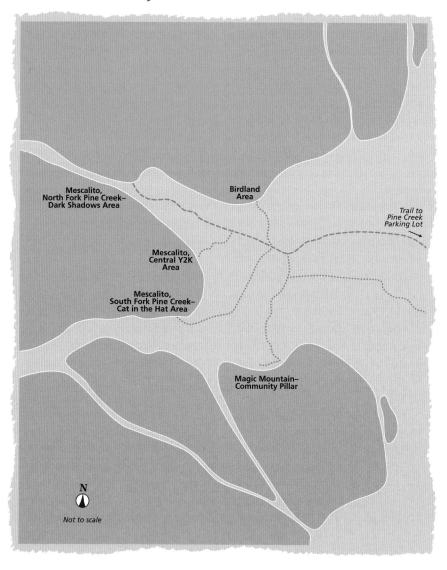

Mescalito,
North Fork Pine Creek–
Dark Shadows Area

Birdland
Area

Trail to
Pine Creek
Parking Lot

Mescalito,
Central Y2K
Area

Mescalito,
South Fork Pine Creek–
Cat in the Hat Area

Magic Mountain–
Community Pillar

N

Not to scale

8.

Pine Creek Canyon

Pine Creek Canyon is at the heart of Las Vegas traditional rock climbing on the Red Rock Canyon Scenic Drive. Dozens of stellar multi-pitch routes wander up the peaks and walls throughout the area. Indeed, there is so much rock that there are literally hundreds of potential unclimbed lines still hidden deep in the canyon. There are enough lines in the area that the parking lot is often full of climbers at 6:30 a.m. Inevitably the climbers wander from car to car as each party racks up—headlamps lit—and compare notes with one another. They realize that they're all headed to the same place and then begin an early morning jog to be first on route, everybody sure that they're faster than the next party. Sometimes the party that gets to the route first is faster, and sometimes not. But they did get there first, and the local ethic dictates that the first to arrive at a given route gets priority. However, the local ethic also dictates that if a party is moving significantly faster than you on a climb, you should give them leeway to pass.

Approach: Enter the Red Rock Canyon Scenic Drive and go 10.4 miles to the parking area on the right side of the road.

BIRDLAND AREA

The Birdland area is a fun multi-pitch venue with a few moderate routes. In the early 2000s this area was completely ignored, and you could climb any route any time, but then word got out . . . Today this is one of those places that often has lines at the base. Plan your day accordingly.

Approach: Drop down the main trail from the Pine Creek parking lot and continue past the old homestead. Approximately 25 minutes from the car, the trail turns sharply right under a large red boulder (this is at the far end of the red cliffband above the trail on the right). This sharp turn leads up to the top of the red cliffband. Near a large boulder perched on the edge of the cliff, a trail works its way up through the boulders on the left. Follow this until it emerges from the boulders onto a steep open hill. Follow the trail up past many cairns to the base of the wall. Often it's a bit easier to access by going up under the little boulder/cave at the end of the trail. Birdland is the obvious crack system directly above the boulder/cave. **Time:** 40 minutes.

Sun Exposure: The Birdland wall is in the sun all day. The Bighorn route goes into the shade in the afternoon.

Types of Climbing Available: Moderate multi-pitch trad climbing

1. Rawlpindi (5.7, II, 550 feet, trad) The first two pitches of this line were originally named Pazookieland after the wonderful BJ's brewery treat. The name was changed after two additional pitches were added to the original ascent. **Pitch 1:** Start on a nice ledge just up and left of Birdland. This route follows the obvious cleft to the left of that route. Ascend the crack up to what looks like an overhanging offwidth. Bypass this on the left. It is not as hard as it looks and is easily protectable. Build a belay station above this at two small bushes (5.7, 150 feet). **Pitch 2:** Continue up and left, bypassing a second small roof. This is the crux of the pitch. After this section the climbing eases to low 5th class. Ascend to a large ledge where it is possible to look down at the belay station at the top of the second pitch of Birdland. You will be directly under the Bighorn hand crack. Build an anchor here (5.7, 150 feet). **Pitch 3:** Things are a bit more runout on pitches 3 and 4. Continue to a bolt, working up at a rightward angle. Climb up a ledge and crack system to a thinner face that wanders up through a series of pockets. Clip a second bolt and then sprint up to the bolted anchor and a hanging stance (5.7, 150 feet). **Pitch**

Birdland Area

Birdland

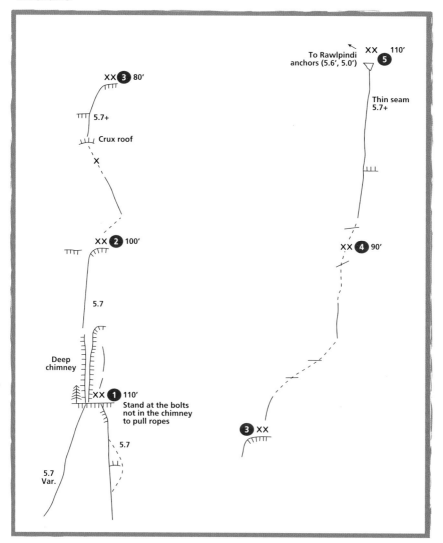

To Rawlpindi anchors (5.6′, 5.0′)

XX **5** 110′

Thin seam 5.7+

XX **3** 80′

5.7+

Crux roof

X

XX **2** 100′

5.7

XX **4** 90′

Deep chimney

XX **1** 110′
Stand at the bolts not in the chimney to pull ropes

3 XX

5.7

5.7
Var.

4: Blast up and right following the crack system to a face. Continue up the face to a bolted anchor (5.7, 100 feet). **Descent:** Rappel pitches 3 and 4 with double ropes. Drop down to the anchor at the top of the second pitch of Birdland and continue to make double-rope rappels to the ground from there. Pro to 4 inches. **FA:** Jason Martin and Marie Dybala, pitches 1 and 2, 2005; Karl and Heidi Wilcox, pitches 3 and 4, 2006.

2. The Big Horn (5.8, II, 420 feet, trad) Bighorn is the beautiful hand crack that slices up the black varnish above the second pitch of Rawlpindi. This is a great option to finish out the day after climbing one of the other routes. There are two options to get to this route. Either climb the first two pitches of Rawlpindi to get to the base, or climb the first two pitches of Birdland and then make a third easy, traversing pitch on the ledge to the base of the route. Climb the beautiful crack to a ledge. Rappel with double ropes. Pro to 4 inches. **FA:** Joe and Betsy Herbst, Matt McMackin, and Randal Grandstaff.

3. Birdland (5.7+, II+, 600 feet, trad) This über-popular route is über fun! **Pitch 1:** Follow the right-hand crack up toward the small roof. Before reaching the roof, cut off to the right and climb around it. Rejoin the crack above the roof. Climb up to a double-bolt anchor at a brushy ledge (5.6, 110 feet). Variation: Climb the left-hand crack instead (5.7). **Pitch 2:** Climb the small crack and the face above the belay. Continue up the crack system to the next ledge and another bolted anchor (5.7, 110 feet). Variation: An equally good option, also 5.7, is to move the belay to the base of the chimney and climb the chimney direct, rejoining the previous option 50 feet up. **Pitch 3:** Move up to the right and climb a left-leaning ramp. Clip a bolt just left of the top of the

ramp and continue to traverse left. Pull a steep move and continue up the crack system. As the system peters out, move up and right to the bolted belay station (5.7+, 80 feet). **Pitch 4:** Climb up right of the anchor and follow a rightward-trending discontinuous crack system to the next anchor. Keep your eyes open for the belay bolts, as they seem to appear out of nowhere. The best way to deal with this pitch is to aim for the small roof up and right. The bolts should appear long before you reach the roof (5.6, 90 feet). **Pitch 5:** Move up and right, working toward the crack that cuts through the left side of the roof. High on the pitch, the crack tightens up and becomes a seam (5.7+, 110 feet). **Descent:** The route can be rappelled with a single 70-meter rope. If you are using a 60-meter rope or shorter, you will need two ropes. On Pitch 2, rappel to the anchors, not to the flat spot below the chimney. Be careful, this is a notorious spot for ropes to get stuck. **Note:** If there are a number of parties below congesting the hanging stances, it is possible to do one more loose pitch with minimal protection, up and to the left, and then rappel Rawlpindi. Traverse out left from the top of pitch 5, protecting wherever possible. Pull through a small loose roof and continue up to the double-bolt anchor at the top of Rawlpindi (5.6, 50 feet). Pro to 4 inches. **FA:** Mark Limage and Chris Burton, 2001.

MESCALITO

It should surprise exactly no one that the Mescalito was named in the late 1960s. Jeff Lansing made the first ascent of this beautiful little cone of a mountain in 1968. And since then literally dozens of routes have gone up on the peak.

The descriptions of the routes here are broken into three major areas: North Fork Pine Creek, Central, and South Fork Pine Creek.

Types of Climbing Available: Multi-pitch face and crack climbing

Mescalito—
North Fork Pine Creek

Approach: From the Pine Creek trailhead, follow the main trail for 20 to 30 minutes until it works its way up a red rock band near a giant boulder. Continue to follow the trail along the rock band until the trail cuts back down to the creek. The trail ends at a stance next to running water and the base of the Dark Shadows wall. **Time:** 40 minutes.

Sun Exposure: Dark Shadows and Chasing Shadows are in the shade all day.

1. Dark Shadows (5.8, II+–IV, 350–1,000 feet, trad) Dark Shadows follows a beautiful corner system above the North Fork of Pine Creek. Historically most people only climbed to the top of the fourth pitch. But if you're looking for adventure, a longer day, and a complex descent, it's a lot of fun to climb Dark Shadows to a large ledge at the top of Perception Tower. **Pitch 1:** Step across the creek and work up the easy face, passing two bolts to an anchor (5.5, 70 feet). **Pitch 2:** Continue up the right-facing corner to a small roof and then traverse down and left to an anchor (5.6, 75 feet). Pitches 1 and 2 can be combined. **Pitch 3:** Blast up the beautiful corner to another bolted anchor. Beware, the crux is at the bottom of the pitch, and there have been a few broken ankles here (5.8, 110 feet). **Pitch 4:** Follow the crack system that arches out to another double-bolt anchor (5.8, 75 feet). **Optional Descent:** Many parties descend from this point. Rappel straight down Chasing Shadows with a single 60-meter rope. After two rappels, you will rejoin Dark Shadows for the final two rappels at the top of pitch 2. Expect your rope to get wet when you pull it from the final rappel. **Pitch 5:** Clip the bolt and then continue up. Climb through an easy roof and then follow the leftward-leaning crack system. Climb up the chimney or stay on the face to a ledge with a double-bolt anchor. As of this writing the bolts were rusty and old. A gear anchor is recommended (5.7, 120 feet). **Pitch 6:** Continue up the chimney and climb through a small roof. Find a bolt approximately 30 feet up and a piton approximately 60 feet up. Work up and left to a bolted anchor at the base of a crack (5.7, 125 feet). **Pitch 7:** Climb the crack,

Mescalito—North Fork Pine Creek

To the upper pitches of Dark Shadows. Most parties rappel from the top of pitch 4.

PHOTO BY ANDY STEPHEN

working up and right. Build an anchor at a varnished stance below another small roof. **Pitch 8:** Climb up right of the roof and work up a hand crack to a series of bushy ledges. Climb to the higher of the ledges and belay below a crack system (5.7, 75 feet). **Pitch 9:** Continue up the crack system to another varnished stance with a single bolt (5.7, 115 feet). **Pitch 10:** Continue up the right-facing corner; as this peters out, work up the face and through the juggy roof. Continue up a low-angle hand crack to the giant tree ledge at the top of Perception Tower (5.8, 175 feet). **Note 1:** The terrain is complex from pitch 5 to the top. If you get lost, just follow the path of least resistance. **Note 2:** Plan adequately for this big day. Over the years several parties have underestimated the size of this climb, and some of those have even been forced to bivy. **Note 3:** Some parties do elect to summit. There are several options, with most requiring approximately two additional pitches of climbing. **Descent:** Walk climber's right to the notch. Drop down slabs toward the North Fork of Pine Creek. Make three double-rope rappels (can be done with a single 70-meter rope) down chimneys and gullies. This will ultimately plant you upstream of the base of Dark Shadows. Pro to 4 inches. **FA:** John Martinet and Nick Nordblom, 1979.

2. Chasing Shadows (5.9, II+, 350 feet, trad) This is a variation to pitches 3 and 4 on Dark Shadows. **Pitches 1 and 2:** Climb the first two pitches of Dark Shadows. **Pitch 3:** Blast up the right-hand crack system up and right of the Pitch 2 anchor (5.8+, 75 feet). **Pitch 4:** Continue up just left of the arête and clip two bolts. Traverse right above a roof and clip an additional bolt. Continue up and eventually back left to the shared anchor for Dark Shadows, Chasing Shadows, and Edge Dressing (5.8+, 95 feet). Pro to 4 inches. **FA:** Randy Marsh and Pier Locatelli, 1990.

3. Edge Dressing (5.10b, II+, 350 feet, mixed) This is a variation for a variation! Climb the first three pitches of Chasing Shadows/Dark Shadows. Instead of cutting right after clipping two bolts on the final pitch of Chasing Shadows, continue up the bolt line to the shared anchor. The route starts easy and gets progressively harder as you work your way up. Pro to 4 inches. **FA:** Randy Marsh and Pier Locatelli, 1993.

Mescalito—Central

The routes listed here are primarily on the right-hand side of the east face or on the northeast face as it wraps around above the North Fork Pine Creek drainage.

Approach: From the Pine Creek parking area, follow the main trail. After walking for 20 to 30 minutes, the main trail makes a right-hand turn and works its way up a red rock band near a giant boulder. Do not follow the trail as it cuts up and right. Instead, follow a spur trail down into the creek. There are a number of variations here. As such, you will either pass by the North Fork of Pine Creek while walking in the creek bed, or you will cross the North Fork of Pine Creek and drop into the South Fork creek bed. Continue to follow the South Fork until an obvious trail cuts up right and out of the bed. Again, there are many variations. Once up on the slope below the Mescalito, follow braided trails, aiming for the center of the mountain. Pauligk Pillar is found to the right of the center of the mountain in a massive right-facing corner. **Time:** 35 minutes.

1. Pauligk Pillar (5.7, 275 feet, trad) A fun little route, this line climbs a massive right-facing corner just to the left of Y2K. **Pitch 1:** Work up the corner, passing a belay station covered in tattered slings to a second station (5.7+, 160 feet). **Pitch 2:** Continue up the corner to a brushy ledge. **Descent:** Rappel the route with double ropes. Beware that this climb is a bit of a rope-eater. Pro to 4 inches. **FA:** Randal Grandstaff and Roland Pauligk and his wife, 1981.

2. Y2K (5.10a, II+, 515 feet, mixed) This is a pleasant climb on outstanding rock! The base of the route is just right of Pauligk Pillar, to the right of a 40-foot-tall pink corner and roof. The climb starts on top of a boulder. **Pitch 1:** Move up through 5.8 terrain using a combination of face and crack climbing past five bolts to a roof. Clip the bolt at the roof and then pull through (crux, 5.10a), then continue up a crack, passing one more bolt to the double-bolt anchor (5.10a, 160 feet). **Pitch 2:** Continue up the varnished face. It's a little easier to go left off the anchor (5.6) vs. going right (5.8). Follow the line of least resistance, passing three bolts. Belay at a stance with a double-bolt anchor. **Pitch 3:** Scramble up to the next ledge and then traverse directly right, passing a bolt on the way. Build an anchor in the varnished corner (5.5, 60 feet). **Pitch 4:** Climb straight up the corner, stemming at the top as it gets harder. From the ledge, step left and scramble up to the top of the line to a double-bolt anchor (5.9, 130 feet). **Descent:** Rappel directly down to the top of pitch 2 with a double-rope rappel. This rappel is a bit of a rope-eater. Make two more double-rope rappels straight down to the ground. Pro to 2 inches, including some micro-nuts for the final pitch. **FA:** Todd Swain and Paul Ross, 1988.

Pauligk Pillar and Y2K

PHOTO BY ANDREW YASSO

PHOTO BY LARRY DeANGELO

Mescalito—
South Fork Pine Creek

The south fork of Pine Creek is the left-hand drainage below the Mescalito.

Approach: From the Pine Creek parking area, follow the main trail. After walking for 20 to 30 minutes, the main trail makes a right-hand turn and works its way up a red rock band near a giant boulder. Do not follow the trail as it cuts up and right. Instead, follow a spur trail down into the creek. There are a number of variations here. As such, you will either pass by the North Fork of Pine Creek while walking in the creek bed, or you will cross the North Fork of Pine Creek and drop into the South Fork creek bed. Continue to follow the South Fork until an obvious trail cuts up right and out of the bed. Again, there are many variations. There is a rocky trail that works its way out of the creek bed just past the North Fork of Pine Creek that will get you there. However, a second trail about 100 yards up the creek is far more pleasant. Each of these trails cuts up right and eventually converges on a well-worn climber's trail. This trail eventually works its way around the southern corner of the Mescalito. Once around the corner, continue up a steep trail to the base of the Cat in the Hat route. **Time:** 45 minutes.

Sun Exposure: The base of Cat in the Hat is shaded in the winter. In the spring and summer, the whole route, base-to-top, is in the blistering sun.

1. Cat in the Hat (5.6+, II+, 510 feet, trad) The best climb of its grade in the conservation area! **Pitch 1:** Ascend the crack system until it terminates only to restart again on the right. Climb up to the right and note the bolted anchor. Do not stop here. Instead, continue up the wide crack to the left until you reach a large triangular ledge. Build an anchor here. Note the rappel anchors up and to the right for the descent, but do not belay at them (5.6+, 150 feet). **Pitch 2:** From the triangular corner, climb directly up the crack in the corner through a small low-5th-class offwidth/chimney. Approximately 20 feet up is a large ledge. Scramble right across easy terrain on the ledge to a small tree. Build an anchor in the crack near the tree (5.6, 60 feet). **Pitch 3:** Continue up the corner. Note the tree with rap slings on it. This is a rappel anchor; do not belay at the tree. Continue up past the tree to a small ledge with several cracks for a traditional anchor (5.5, 70 feet). **Pitch 4:** Follow cracks up to a roof. It is possible to climb directly over the roof, but the crack system to the left provides easier climbing and better protection. Once beyond here the difficulty eases. Continue up the crack system until it becomes a gully. Climb up to the right and onto a ledge with a big boulder wrapped in

Cat in the Hat

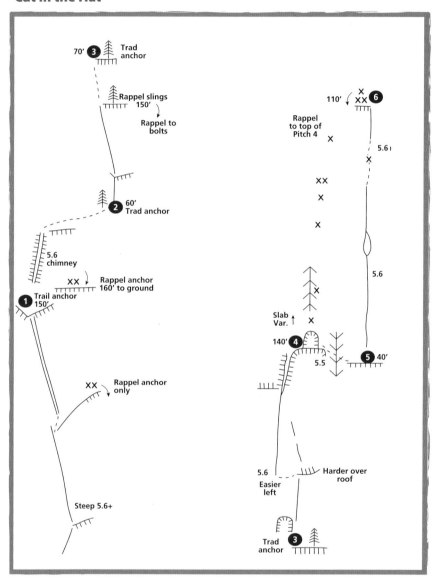

70' **3** Trad anchor

Rappel slings 150'
Rappel to bolts

2 60' Trad anchor

5.6 chimney

XX Rappel anchor 160' to ground

1 Trail anchor 150'

XX Rappel anchor only

Steep 5.6+

110' **6**
Rappel to top of Pitch 4

5.6 I

XX

X

X

5.6

Slab Var.

140' **4**

5.5

5 40'

5.6
Easier left

Harder over roof

Trad anchor **3**

webbing (5.6, 140 feet). **Pitch 5:** Drop down 10 feet and traverse right. Build an anchor on the enclosed ledge next to the cave (5.5, 40 feet). **Pitch 6:** Lead up a beautiful crack system to a slab. Clip the bolt (crux) and then work up to the next crack system and the top of the line (5.6+, 110 feet). **Descent:** Rappel the line with double ropes. Rappel straight down the bolted arête to the top of pitch 4. Continue to make double-rope rappels until you reach the ground. **Note:** The bolted arête above pitch 4 is 5.10b. Pro to 3 inches. **FA:** Bruce Eisner and Joanne Urioste, 1976.

Magic Mountain— Community Pillar

The chimneys and tunnels on Tunnel Vision impress many people. But Tunnel Vision ain't got nothin' on Community Pillar. This is a route where entire pitches take place inside the mountain!

If you like this kind of climbing, don't miss the aforementioned Tunnel Vision (see the "Angel Food Wall" chapter). Obviously, you should climb Community Pillar; you should also consider Black Dagger (see the "Juniper Canyon" chapter), and, of course, you should definitely climb Epinephrine (see the "Black Velvet Canyon" chapter). These four routes comprise the most interesting tunnel and chimney climbs in Red Rock Canyon National Conservation Area.

Approach: From the Pine Creek parking area, follow the main trail just past the foundation of the old house. Cut left on the Oak Creek Canyon Trail. As the trail begins to work back east, spot one of the braided climber's trails and follow it up to the base of the face. **Time:** 35 minutes.

Sun Exposure: Community Pillar is in the shade all day.

Types of Climbing Available: Chimney, crack, and tunnel climbing— all trad

1. Community Pillar (5.9, IV, 800 feet, trad) There are a number of variations on this route, and it is reasonable to believe that an individual could climb this line several ways and have a very different experience each time. **Pitch 1:** Climb up the back of the wide chimney and tunnel behind the chockstone. This is a very tight squeeze; indeed, there are stories about people stripping their harnesses of gear and shoving it through. (5.9, 100 feet). Variations: There is a chimney to the left of the chockstone that can be used to bypass the squeeze. Alternatively, some people will climb up and around the chockstone on the left. **Pitch 2:** Continue up the crack system on the right. The climbing will become easier. Work up 4th-class terrain to the base of a chimney (5.8, 150 feet). **Note:** Some people break this into two shorter pitches. **Pitch 3:** Work up the

Magic Mountain-Community Pillar

The rest of the climb is hidden inside the mountain and up behind the visible features.

Var.

Rappel Route

PHOTO BY LARRY DEANGELO

chimney and squeeze past another giant chockstone. Belay on top of the chockstone (5.6, 80 feet). **Pitch 4:** Climb the offwidth crack on the right-hand side until it changes into a tunnel. Continue up inside and escape out of a hole on the left-hand side of the tunnel. Build a belay on the ledge (5.8+, 130 feet). Variation: Climb the left-hand hand and fist crack to belay at the same ledge (5.9, 130 feet). **Pitch 5:** Continue up the crack on the left with a combination of face and crack climbing. Climb up to a cave. Chimney and make your way to the back. Build a belay here (5.7, 100 feet). **Pitch 6:** Jam up the crack and offwidth at the back of the cave until you are nearly at the top. There is a small cave behind you with two exits. Take the climber's left exit and belay there (5.8, 90 feet). Variation: Climb the crack on the outside of the chimney (5.9, 120 feet). **Pitch 7:** Exit the chimney and then continue up on the face on terrain that continually becomes easier (5.0, 160 feet). **Descent:** Scramble climber's right to a small cave, then work down the cave. Alternatively, you can rappel off a pine tree, but there is a lot of loose rock and it's much more dangerous. Scramble down to the west toward a notch separating Magic Mountain from the Magic Triangle. Make five single-rope rappels. Pro to 4 inches. **FA:** Joe Herbst and Tom Kaufman, 1976.

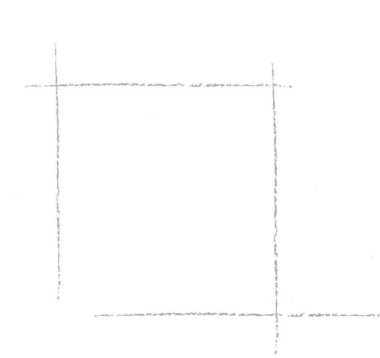

Juniper Canyon

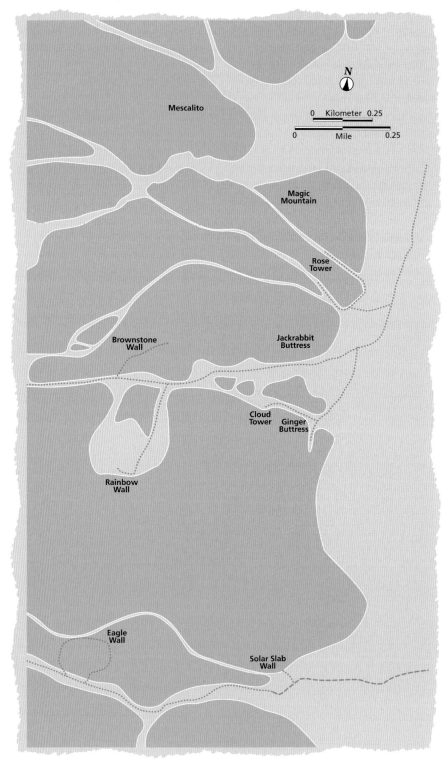

9.

Juniper Canyon

Juniper Canyon is another highly varied climbing destination. The area is composed of the Rose Tower, the Jackrabbit Buttress, the Brownstone Wall, the Rainbow Wall, and the north end of Rainbow Mountain. These are all large sandstone features, and each of them hosts a handful of classic lines!

Approach: All approaches for Juniper Canyon are from the Pine Creek parking area. To get there, take the Red Rock Canyon Scenic Drive for 10.4 miles and park on the right.

ROSE TOWER

The Rose Tower is a pretty piece of rock visible to the right of the Jackrabbit Buttress. The most famous route on the feature is Olive Oil, a six-pitch 5.7, with interesting and varied movement.

Approach: From the Pine Creek parking area, drop down the main trail. A short time after leaving your car, the Fire Ecology Trail appears on the left. Take this trail and follow it across two washes toward the steep

Juniper Canyon Overview

trail that cuts up the hillside. Climb up the steep trail to the top of the hill and follow the trail to a T junction with a sign that has an arrow on it. Go right on this trail. After a few minutes, you come to another junction. Take the right-hand fork down into the wash and back toward Pine Creek Canyon for a moment. After crossing the depression, take the first left-hand trail. Follow braided trails up toward the gully to the left of the Rose Tower. A trail will eventually take you up a tight, brushy gully to the base of Olive Oil. **Time:** 40 minutes.

Sun Exposure: Olive Oil is in the sun all day. The base and the final pitch are mildly shaded.

Rose Tower

PHOTO BY ANDY STEPHEN

Types of Climbing Available: Crack, chimney, and face trad climbing

1. Olive Oil (5.7 R, III, 600 feet, trad) A great route with a few runouts and a very quick descent makes Olive Oil a popular ascent. Climbers should be okay with the runouts, as they're on easier terrain. **Pitch 1:** A short buttress shoots straight up out of an alcove just left of a chimney and into a corner. Climb up this sparsely protected buttress and work into the corner. Belay at a small sandy alcove (5.7 R, 100 feet). **Pitch 2:** Follow the right-facing corner up to a perfect crack. Follow this to a stance (5.7,

Olive Oil

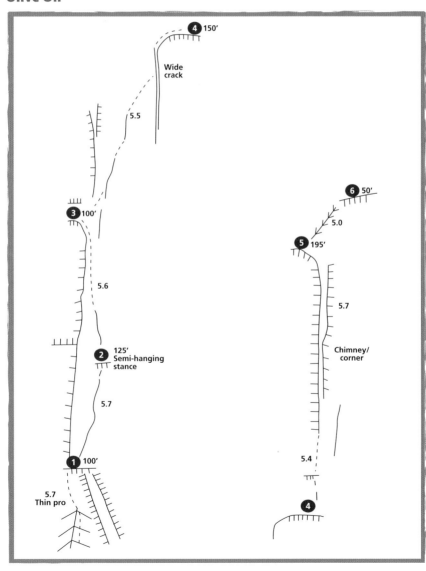

125 feet). **Pitch 3:** Continue to follow a combination of the crack on the face and the corner. Climb to a ledge on the left-hand side (5.6, 100 feet). **Pitch 4:** Follow cracks and face climbing up and to the right. Things get thin here. Continue working up and right toward a large left-facing corner characterized by a wide and deep crack. Follow the crack for a short distance until you can climb up onto a large flat ledge (5.6, 150 feet). **Pitch 5:** Climb up easy terrain to a short, steeper wall and then up into the wide corner. The corner is the crux of the route. Continue working up the corner on this rope-stretcher of a pitch to a stance on the left (5.7, 195 feet). **Pitch 6:** Scramble up and right to the top of the wall (5.0, 50 feet). **Descent:** Walk northwest on a rib to a small step. Drop down the step and work toward the gully on the right. Hike down the gully and contour back around the bottom of the feature to get back to the base of the route. **Note:** This route can easily be done in four pitches with a 70-meter rope. Combine pitches 2 and 3, as well as 5 and 6. Pro to 4 inches. **FA:** John Williamson and Jorge and Joanne Urioste, 1978.

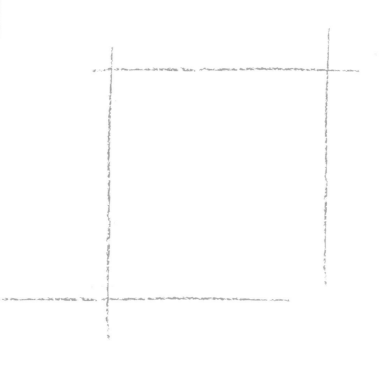

JACKRABBIT BUTTRESS

The Jackrabbit Buttress can be seen just down and to the left of the Rose Tower. And while the buttress isn't one of the larger features in Red Rock, it still sports several routes and harbors many opportunities for first ascents.

Geronimo is one of the few routes in this book that ends on a minor summit. As such, it is also one of the few routes that has a summit register!

Approach: From the Pine Creek parking area, drop down the main trail. A short time after leaving your car, the Fire Ecology Trail appears on the left. Take this trail and follow it across two washes toward the steep trail that cuts up the hillside. Climb up the steep trail to the top of the hill and follow the trail to a T junction with a sign that has an arrow on it. Go right on this trail. After a few minutes, you come to another junction. Take the right-hand fork down into the wash and back toward Pine Creek Canyon for a moment. After crossing the depression, take the first left-hand trail. Follow braided trails up toward the bottom of the buttress. **Time:** 50 minutes.

Sun Exposure: Saddle Up and MysterZ see morning sun in the winter and significantly more sun in the spring and summer. Geronimo is in the sun all day.

Types of Climbing Available: Traditional multi-pitch, face, crack, and chimney climbing

Doug Foust works his way up an awesome crack on Saddle Up.
Photo Andrew Yasso

1. Saddle Up (5.9, II, 590 feet, trad) This line is found on the south end of the Jackrabbit Buttress, in the gully that makes its way up to the Rainbow Wall and the Brownstone Wall. The most obvious landmark for the line is the giant chockstone on the top of pitch 1. Scramble and bushwhack up to an alcove and then scramble up 3rd-class terrain to the base of the route. **Pitch 1:** Stem and chimney up featured rock. As the rock smooths out, climb up a left-slanting rib into a cave system. Stem and chimney up left to gain the top of the chockstone. Build an anchor in the T-shaped crack at your ankles. Note that there are several variations, and the pitch can be climbed at a harder or easier grade (5.7+, 110 feet). **Pitch 2:** Step off the chockstone to the right and out over a void. Make a couple of face moves to gain a steep hand crack on the right. Jam your way up the crack, watching for an occasional jug on the right wall. Continue up past a white flake on the left side of the crack and belay just above (5.9, 120 feet). **Pitch 3:** Continue up the crack as the angle eases. Pass a varnished alcove and belay at a ledge 15 feet above (5.7, 170 feet). **Pitch 4:** Follow the left-trending crack to the end and then angle right (5.4, 200 feet). **Descent:** Unrope and scramble up to the top of the giant gully climber's left, just below the Brownstone Wall. Descend the gully back to the base of the route. Pro to 4 inches. Some parties may want a 5-inch piece for the first pitch. **FA:** Doug Foust and Andrew Yasso, 2013.

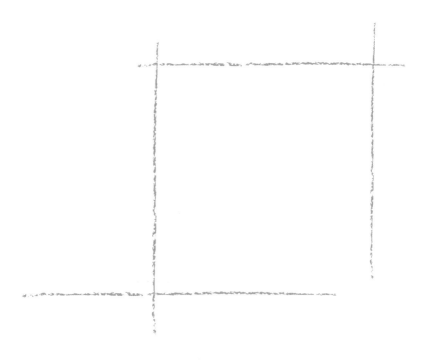

Jackrabbit Buttress

PHOTO BY DOUG FOUST

Jackrabbit Buttress

To Saddle Up (in the shade),
Brownstone Wall,
and Rainbow Wall

2

2. MysterZ (5.7, III, 1,100 feet, trad)
This route was named for the memory of Zack Martin, a climber who tragically died in a car accident in 2003. There are two ribs to the Jackrabbit Buttress. MysterZ is found on the left-hand rib to the left of the gully that separates the ribs. Geronimo is on the right-hand rib. The first pitch of MysterZ starts up a wide crack/chimney just to the right of the shield of rock that denotes the bottom of the left-hand rib. **Pitch 1:** Climb up the chimney. It slowly pinches off to become a crack and then opens up to be a chimney again. Belay at the first stance above the pinch inside the chimney (5.7, 160 feet). **Pitch 2:** Continue up out of the chimney to a scoop. Step across and follow the hand crack to a slanting ledge below zebra-striped rock (5.6, 150 feet). **Pitch 3:** Traverse up left on the zebra-striped rock to a tree at the base of a black crack (3rd class, 190 feet). **Pitch 4:** Climb the black finger crack. At the top there is a rock on a pedestal. Belay at the stance to the right (5.6, 165 feet). **Pitch 5:** Climb up and left into the giant flare, passing a bush. Stem up and follow the chimney as it pinches down to a crack. Traverse to the right at the top, but do not go up the overhanging chimney. Climb up another exposed black crack to a series of horizontal cracks and build a

Jackrabbit Buttress

3 Bottom of route hidden behind this feature

Geronimo

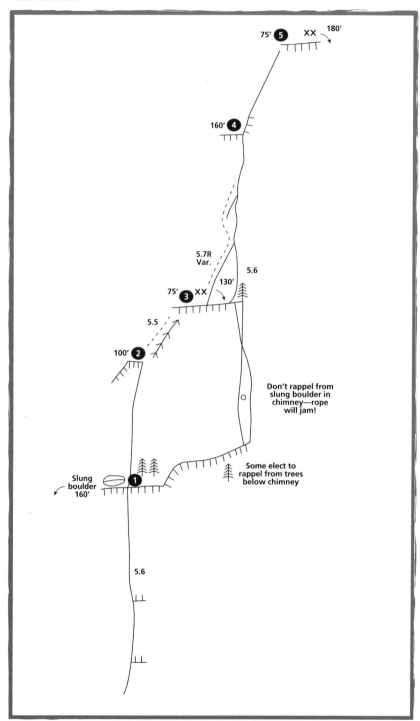

75' **5** ✕✕ 180'

160' **4**

5.7R
Var.

5.6

75' **3** ✕✕ 130'

5.5

100' **2**

Don't rappel from
slung boulder in
chimney—rope
will jam!

Some elect to
rappel from trees
below chimney

Slung
boulder
160'

1

5.6

belay (5.7, 170 feet). **Pitch 6:** Continue up an easy crack. The terrain continues to get lower angled and easier the higher you climb. Build a belay at a stance (5.4, 190 feet). Pitch 7 and 8: Though there might be a 5th-class move here or there, the climbing mostly eases to 3rd class to the top of the feature. **Descent:** Scramble up to the base of the Brownstone Wall, then scramble down the gully to the left. Continue down the main gully, climber's left (south) of the Jackrabbit Buttress. Pro to 4 inches. **FA:** Jimmy Newberry and Phil Broscovak, 2003.

3: Geronimo (5.6, II, 570 feet, trad) There are two ribs to the Jackrabbit Buttress. Geronimo is found on the right-hand rib to the right of the gully that separates the ribs. The base of the route is up a small gully and starts in an obvious crack. **Pitch 1:** Ascend a long pitch up the obvious crack to a large ledge (5.6, 160 feet). **Pitch 2:** Cross the ledge and climb through some bushes to the second crack system. Ascend this crack for 100 feet. Build an anchor at the small platform (5.6, 100 feet). If you have a 60-meter rope, it is possible to combine pitches 2 and 3. **Pitch 3:** Climb the face (thin placements) up to bolts on the next large ledge (5.5, 75 feet). **Pitch 4:** Ascend the right crack—the left crack is runout 5.6—up to a small platform. Continue up the crack and corner as it veers to the left. Build an anchor in the corner of the smallish ledge. Beware of the loose flake in the back of the crack (5.6, 160 feet). **Pitch 5:** Climb up and left for 5 feet and then traverse right across a ledge. Continue up the somewhat exposed arête. Belay at the descent bolts (5.6, 75 feet). **Descent:** Make a double-rope (180-foot) rappel from the bolts to the platform at the top of pitch 2. Make a second double-rope (170-foot) rappel from bolts to the large ledge at the top of pitch 1. Make a final double-rope (160-foot) rappel from equalized slings on the boulder. When rappelling, be sure that the rope stays out of the crack and that it lays in the best place for the knot to descend the wall. Geronimo is notorious for stuck ropes. Pro to 4 inches. **FA:** Bill and Michelle Cramer, 1992.

BROWNSTONE WALL

The Brownstone Wall is the beautiful broad wall that sits above the Jackrabbit Buttress. Due to the approach, the lines up here don't see as much action as other lines in the area, but that doesn't mean there aren't several quality routes. Indeed, many local climbers believe The Nightcrawler to be one of the overall best routes in the entirety of Red Rock!

Approach: There are two options for the approach. The first option is to climb either Saddle Up or MysterZ to reach the bottom of the wall. The second option is to approach as for the Jackrabbit Buttress. Skirt around the left-hand side of the buttress and then climb up the steep gully to the base of the Brownstone Wall. **Time:** 2 hours.

Sun Exposure: The Brownstone Wall is in the sun most of the day. Routes on the left-hand side of the wall, like the Black Dagger, go into shade early in the winter.

Types of Climbing Available: Crack, face, and chimney multi-pitch trad climbing

1. Black Dagger (5.7+ R, III+, 700 feet, trad) This line is found on the far left side of the Brownstone Wall. The base of the route is just up and right of the approach gully. To find the line, locate the overhang on the second pitch and the crack system above. The route climbs a right-facing corner system. Scramble up 200 feet of lower-angled rock to the base of the route proper. **Pitch 1:** Climb up a crack to a block below a white roof (5.6, 120

Brownstone Wall

The left side of the Brownstone Wall

Tunnel Behind

feet). **Pitch 2:** Traverse left, then climb up to a crack on the left-hand side of the roof. It is a bit runout beyond the roof. Work back right on plates to the main right-facing corner system. Continue up this to a ledge below a large corner (5.7+, 140 feet). **Pitch 3:** Hope you remembered the big gear! If you didn't, this pitch could be quite runout. Climb up the beautiful varnished corner to the fat crack. Stem and face climb up the corner to the base of a smooth chimney (5.7+, 130 feet). **Pitch 4:** Blast up the easy—but very deep—chimney. Exit left through a hole and onto a huge ledge at the top of a pillar (5.0, 80 feet). **Pitch 5:** Continue up the plated face to a low-angle, right-facing corner. Climb up to the highest ledge below a roof (5.6, 100 feet). **Pitch 6:** Work up the face to the roof. Climb through the roof and then follow a right-facing corner to a large ledge (5.6, 120 feet). **Descent:** Scramble up to the top of the wall and then descend climber's left (south) toward the Gunsight Notch. Drop down the notch and descend the gully back toward the base of the wall. There are a few short 5th-class sections that can be rappelled or downclimbed. **Note:** After it snows, all of the snow that hits the Rainbow Wall sheds down into the Gunsight Notch descent. This option should not be attempted when there is snow in the descent gully. It often freezes and becomes a dangerous sheet of ice that requires dozens of rappels. Pro

to 5 inches. It is recommended that you have two to four very large pieces for the third pitch. **FA:** Joe Herbst and Rick Wheeler, 1977.

2. The Nightcrawler (5.10c, III+, 485 feet, mixed) A deep gully separates the north end from the south end of the Brownstone Wall. The south end protrudes a bit more than the rest of the wall to the left of this gully. Approximately 200 feet to the left of that is a pillar commonly referred to as the Hourglass. The Nightcrawler climbs up the right-hand side of the Hourglass, sending a massive right-facing corner. The base of the line starts on a brushy ledge approximately 40 feet up. **Pitch 1:** Climb up easy cracks on the right side of the Hourglass. Work up these at a slightly leftward angle for approximately 140 feet. At the top, traverse left toward a bolted anchor (5.7, 150 feet). This pitch could be longer if you choose to start a bit lower than the recommended ledge start. **Pitch 2:** Climb into the right-facing crack that quickly opens up into a chimney. As the chimney terminates, move right across the face to another right-facing crack. The pitch ends on a ledge with a double-bolt anchor (5.9, 120 feet). **Pitch 3:** Climb a combination of the fist crack on the left and the finger crack on the right. The crack on the right will eventually fade. This pitch has seven bolts, but small gear is required to supplement them. The pitch ends at

Brownstone Wall

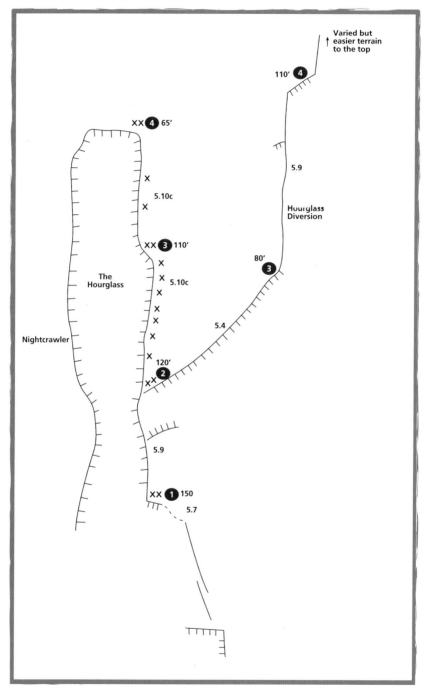

a ledge with a double-bolt anchor (5.10c, 110 feet). **Pitch 4:** Continue up the beautiful splitter crack in the corner system using a combination of jamming and liebacking. There are two bolts on this pitch, and it ends at a double-bolt belay at the top of the Hourglass (5.10c, 65 feet). **Descent:** Rappel the route with double ropes. Beware of the rope-eating crack at the top, and don't try to combine rappels. Many parties rappel to the top of the second pitch and then continue climbing up the wall via the Hourglass Diversion. Pro to 4 inches. **FA:** Jorge and Joanne Urioste, 1978.

3. Hourglass Diversion (5.9, III+, 700 feet, trad) This line is often overlooked because of the quality of the route next door. But it is well worth climbing and can be an excellent way to round out the day after climbing The Nightcrawler. **Pitches 1 and 2:** Climb the first two pitches of The Nightcrawler. **Pitch 3:** Traverse up and right on the ramp to the base of a thin crack and build an anchor. Beware of bird poo on this pitch (5.4, 80 feet). **Pitch 4:** Continue up the thin crack. There is a minor ledge at approximately 80 feet, but a much better ledge is found at approximately 110 feet (5.9, 110 feet). **Pitches 5 and 6:** Continue to the top of the feature following the crack system. There is approximately 240 feet of varied but continually easier climbing to the top. Break the pitches into appropriate

lengths to avoid rope drag (5.8, 240 feet). **Descent:** Scramble up to the top of the wall and then descend climber's left (south) toward the Gunsight Notch. Drop down the notch and descend the gully back toward the base of the wall. There are a few short 5th-class sections that can be rappelled or downclimbed. **Note:** After it snows, all of the snow that hits the Rainbow Wall sheds down into the Gunsight Notch descent. This option should not be attempted when there is snow in the descent gully. It often freezes and becomes a dangerous sheet of ice that requires dozens of rappels. Pro to 4 inches. **FA:** John Rosholt and Jorge and Joanne Urioste, 1978.

4. Armatron (5.9, III+, 600 feet, trad) This fantastic route is found significantly to the right of The Nightcrawler, right of the break in the center of the Brownstone Wall. As you move across the base of the wall from the break, look for a large patch of broken varnish in the tan rock at the base of a giant pillar. The first pitch of the route climbs up the center of the varnished face. **Pitch 1:** Climb up the face, passing five bolts until you reach a scoop on the left (5.8, 100 feet). **Pitch 2:** Continue up a finger crack and then step right to another crack. Eventually you will reach the base of a massive left-facing corner. Do not work up the corner. Instead, step right and clip a bolt. Climb up

Brownstone Wall

Photo by Andy Stephen

Descent

into the varnish and build an anchor at a double-bolt belay (5.9, 165 feet). **Pitch 3:** This beautiful pitch climbs directly up chocolate-plated rock to a double-bolt anchor (5.6, 160 feet). **Pitch 4:** Work up left from the belay, following more plated varnish. Step right to another belay station (5.6, 100 feet). **Pitch 5:** Follow the arête, passing three bolts to an anchor on the Humerus Ledge (5.7, 120 feet). **Pitch 6:** Continue up and left, climbing a wide corner and crack. Bypass a roof on the left and then follow a finger crack. After the finger crack terminates, continue up the runout face to the top of the tower and a small summit (5.8, 130 feet). **Descent:** Scramble to the top of the peak. Some people may want a rope to finish this scramble, as there are a few exposed areas. From the summit, traverse north over a white secondary summit to a large tree on the north side of the summit plateau. Follow cairns to a spot that appears to cliff out. Downclimb through a small tunnel on skier's right. Continue to follow cairns down to the base of the wall. Pro to 2 inches. You may want extra wires for pitch 3. **FA:** Geoff Conley, Jimmy Newberry, Jeffrey Johnson, and Jorge and Joanne Urioste, 2003.

RAINBOW WALL

Perched behind Rainbow Mountain and south of the Brownstone Wall, the Rainbow Wall is one of the most striking features in Red Rock Canyon. Joe Herbst and Larry Hamilton completed the first ascent of the Rainbow Wall in 1973 via the Original Route. The party used a combination of free and aid techniques to make their way up.

In 1994 Leo Henson added several bolts to the route and made the first free ascent. Many traditionalists disliked the fact that the line now had a pile of bolts on it, and a large number of them were chopped.

Dan McQuade—who was on the second free ascent team—returned to the wall and replaced many of the missing bolts. However, he did not replace them all. This stripped-down version of the climb seemed to appease the traditionalists, and it is what climbers will find on the wall today.

The bulk of the climbers that visit the Original Route on the Rainbow Wall today are free climbers. However, a small group of aid climbers still occasionally make ascents. If you are interested in completing an aid ascent of the route, it is imperative that you (1) only use clean gear, (2) only climb the route when it is bone dry, (3) try to avoid the use of cam hooks, as they damage the sandstone, and (4) respect free climbers and allow them to pass.

Approach: From the Pine Creek parking area, drop down the main trail. A short time after leaving your car, the Fire Ecology Trail appears on the left. Take this trail and follow it across two washes toward the steep trail that cuts up the hillside. Climb up the steep trail to the top of the hill and follow the trail to a T junction with a sign that has an arrow on it. Go right on this trail. After a few minutes, you come to another junction. Take the right-hand fork down into the wash and back toward Pine Creek Canyon for a moment. After crossing the depression, take the first left-hand trail. Follow braided trails up toward the bottom of the Jackrabbit Buttress. Contour around the base of the buttress and climb up the gully between Rainbow Mountain and the Jackrabbit Buttress. Eventually you will reach a steep, water-polished slab/gully on the left below the Rainbow Wall. Climb up this slab (5.0) to the bowl beneath the Rainbow Wall. There is commonly a fixed line here. Continue up to the base of the wall. **Time:** 2 to 3 hours.

Sun Exposure: The Rainbow Wall is mostly in the shade all day. In the spring through early fall, the wall is in the sun in the early morning.

Types of Climbing Available: Hard multi-pitch free climbing or moderate aid climbing. Crack, slab, face, and steep terrain, it's all there.

Original Route

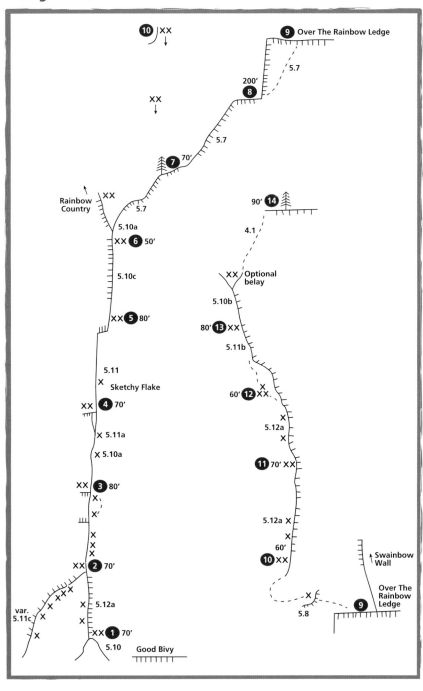

1. Original Route (5.12a or 5.10a C2, V, 1,200 feet, mixed) This beautiful line is found smack dab in the center of the massive Rainbow Wall. The line starts approximately 100 feet left of the giant red arches at a perfectly flat ledge below the giant corner. This ledge is commonly used for a bivy. **Pitch 1:** Begin in the corner and climb up easy terrain to a bolted anchor below a steep crack (5.6, 70 feet). **Pitch 2:** Blast up the crack and into the black corner, passing two bolts. Make a big, reachy 5.12 move to attain the bolted anchor (5.12a or 5.7 C2, 70 feet). Variation: Instead of climbing up the 5.6 pitch into the 5.12 pitch, climb the arched bolted line (six bolts) to the left of the standard route's base. This variation joins the Original Route at the top of the second pitch (5.11c, 140 feet). **Pitch 3:** Step up from the anchor and lieback up the crack, passing four bolts until you are forced right, out onto the face. The aid line goes straight up here. Free climbers should work up to the right, passing two more bolts, before stepping back into the corner. Continue up to a bolted belay station on a sloped ledge (5.11d or 5.8 C2, 80 feet). **Pitch 4:** Climb up the corner to another bolted station (5.11a or 5.9 C2, 70 feet). **Pitch 5:** Continue in the corner. Work up a sketchy flake to a bolt. Continue up to a roof and bypass it on the right (5.11b or 5.7 A1, 80 feet). **Pitch 6:** Climb up the right-facing corner to a bolted belay station (5.10c

or A1, 50 feet). **Note:** Many people climb the four-pitch 5.12d Rainbow Country variation here. This variation rejoins the Original Route at the top of pitch 10. **Pitch 7:** Continue up the corner, contouring to the right as a brushy ledge appears. Belay on the ledge (5.10a, 70 feet). **Pitch 8:** Work up the ledge system right, working over "Faith Ledge" and through the "Bat Cave" and up to another ledge below a red left-facing corner; build a belay (5.7, 200 feet). **Pitch 9:** Traverse right around the arête to obtain some awesome exposure. Climb straight up on less-than-awesome rock to reach a bolted anchor on a large spacious ledge (the Over the Rainbow Ledge) (5.7, 80 feet). **Note 1:** Historically, the Over the Rainbow Ledge has been used as a bivy ledge. **Note 2:** You can escape from the Original Route by climbing the Swainbow Wall variation from here. **Pitch 10:** Traverse left, passing a bolt. Climb back into the corner system and step up to a small ledge (5.8, 60 feet). **Pitch 11:** Continue up the huge red left-facing corner, passing two bolts to a bolted anchor. The bouldery crux is at the glue-in bolt. Many consider this the best free pitch (5.12a or C2, 70 feet). **Pitch 12:** Work up the corner, passing two more bolts. Traverse left to a stance and a bolted anchor. The aid line continues straight up (5.12a or C2, 60 feet). **Pitch 13:** There are two options here: (1) Stay left, passing a bolt, and climb up left of the roof, or

(2) downclimb and step left to a small left-facing corner and climb up this until the two lines meet at the roof. Continue up the corner to an anchor on the left (5.11b or C2, 80 feet). **Pitch 14:** Continue up, making a move up a flared crack. Continue up easier ground to the top of the feature. You'll note a bolted belay on your left. It's better just to work up past it on low 5th-class terrain to the top. Belay at a pine tree at the top of the wall (5.10b or C1, 90 feet). **Descent:** The route can be rappelled with a single 60-meter rope from the top of the wall. You will need to search around a little for the anchor with a 60-meter, but it's there. That said, many parties prefer a 70-meter rope as it provides more options. The very first rappel is a real rope-stretcher if you don't pay close attention. Pro to 4 inches, including micro-nuts. **FA:** Joe Herbst and Larry Hamilton, 1973. **FFA:** Leo Henson, 1994.

2. Rainbow Country Variation

(5.12d) This four-pitch variation ups the ante on any free ascent of the Rainbow Wall. Climb the first six pitches of the wall's Original Route to reach it. **Pitch 7:** Instead of cutting right into the ledge system, continue up to the right-facing crack. Climb past the first set of anchors and belay

Rainbow Wall

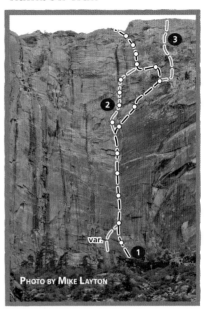

PHOTO BY MIKE LAYTON

at the second. Make sure to use long runners (5.11b, 100 feet). **Pitch 8:** Work up thin moves to a chimney. Climb through the chimney, sending a small roof to a bolted stance (5.11b, 90 feet). **Pitch 9:** Climb through a bulge, working up a thin face to a right-facing corner. Climb past six bolts, through a roof to a bolted anchor. **Pitch 10:** Traverse down and right, passing a bolt. Continue traversing 40 feet to the Original Route's anchors below pitch 11, beneath the red dihedrals (5.12b, 60 feet). **FA:** Dan McQuade and Eric Camillo, 1996.

3. Swainbow Wall Variation (5.10b R/X) This seldom-climbed three-pitch variation is not awesome, but it does provide an easier escape to the top of the Rainbow Wall if needed. The line starts on the Over the Rainbow Ledge. **Pitch 10:** Climb up the shallow left-leaning corner from the center of the Over the Rainbow Ledge. Traverse down and left and then continue up a runout flake. Continue up and then work up through a right-facing corner (crux). Step up to belay at a tree (5.10b, 150 feet). **Pitch 11:** Follow the corner system, passing several ledges. Angle back right to belay at a sloping ledge. The rock here is funky, and it may take a few minutes to build a reasonable anchor (5.7, 170 feet). **Pitch 12:** Blast straight up the steep and intimidating face with almost no pro to the summit. This pitch is R/X (5.5, 90 feet). **FA:** Jeff Rickerl, Mark Hoffman, and Todd Swain, 1992.

CLOUD TOWER

The Cloud Tower area is known for two mega-classics, one moderate and one not-so-moderate. Crimson Chrysalis is one of those super routes that everybody wants to climb. Cloud Tower is also a super route, and everybody wants to climb it too, but it's much harder. The result is that there are often lines for Crimson, but not so much for Cloud Tower.

One of the cruxes of climbing Crimson Chrysalis is determining when to leave the parking lot on a busy day. If you get up first, you'll get to climb fast, but will also have to negotiate crowds on the descent. If you get up late, you'll be at the back of the line, which may or may not be a problem, but everyone above will have to rappel through your party on their way down. There's no perfect answer.

If you hike in to climb Crimson Chrysalis and find that it's super busy, you might consider switching your objective to Ginger Cracks. This route is relatively close and is very similar in character to Crimson. The big difference is that you don't have to rappel the route, which takes some of the pressure off.

Approach: From the Pine Creek parking area, drop down the main trail. A short time after leaving your car, the Fire Ecology Trail appears on the left. Take this trail and follow it across two washes toward the steep trail that cuts up the hillside. Climb up the steep trail to the top of the hill and follow the trail to a T junction with a sign that has an arrow on it. Go right on this trail. After a few minutes, you come to another junction. Take the right-hand fork down into the wash and back toward Pine Creek Canyon for a moment. After crossing the depression, take the first left-hand trail. Follow this trail across the major deep wash that comes out from between Rainbow Mountain and Jackrabbit Buttress. Cross the wash, then turn right on braided trails and work up the giant ramp to the obvious pink tower with the red top on the north end of Rainbow Mountain. Crimson Chrysalis climbs the center of this feature, while the Cloud Tower is just beyond it. **Time:** 1 to 2 hours.

Sun Exposure: Crimson Chrysalis is in the shade all day. If it's windy, this can be a very cold route. The bottom of the Cloud Tower route is in the shade, but the top gets afternoon sun.

Types of Climbing Available: Multi-pitch trad crack and face climbing, with some bolts thrown in for fun

1. Crimson Chrysalis (5.8+, IV, 900 feet, mixed) One of the most well-known routes in the canyon, this is an aesthetic and incredibly exposed route for the grade. The line climbs an awesome crack system for five pitches. As the crack peters out, the route continues up the face to the top of the tower. Start approximately 100 feet beyond the top of the approach ramp in a beautiful crack. **Pitch 1:** Send the crack and the face

Cloud Tower

Cloud Tower

Crimson Chrysalis and Cloud Tower as seen from the wash between Rainbow Mountain and the Jackrabbit Buttress

PHOTO BY MIKE LAYTON

on the right—passing six bolts—to a bolted belay (5.7, 130 feet). **Pitch 2:** Continue working up the same crack and corner, passing five bolts to a bolted belay station (5.8, 90 feet). **Pitch 3:** Climb up the crack and clip a bolt. Work up right, passing two more bolts. Step up to a ledge with a double-bolt anchor (5.8+, 100 feet). **Pitch 4:** Wiggle up a chimney, passing a bolt. Step up to a long thin crack and continue up, passing two bulges to a belay ledge with bolts (5.8, 90 feet). **Pitch 5:** Continue up the hand and finger crack, passing a bolt to another ledge and a double-bolt belay (5.8, 110 feet). **Pitch 6:** Step up and left through a steep section. Clip two bolts and then climb past a ledge, angling right past three more bolts (5.8+, 100 feet). **Pitch 7:** Time to climb the face! Scamper up past nine bolts

to an anchor in the red rock (5.7, 120 feet). **Pitch 8:** Work 25 feet up the red rock to a ramp. Clip a bolt and then traverse 10 feet right. Continue up left on another ramp. Work up past three more bolts to a belay station (5.7, 75 feet). **Pitch 9:** Pull up and right. Clip four bolts and then work through a small roof to attain the top (5.8, 75 feet). **Descent:** Rappel the route with double ropes. Pro to 4 inches. **FA:** Jorge and Joanne Urioste, 1979.

2. Cloud Tower (5.11d, IV, 815 feet, trad) This is not just one of the best climbs of this grade in Red Rock, but is also considered one of the best climbs of this grade in the country! The movement here is absolutely amazing. Cloud Tower is approximately 150 feet beyond the top of the approach ramp to the right of

Cloud Tower

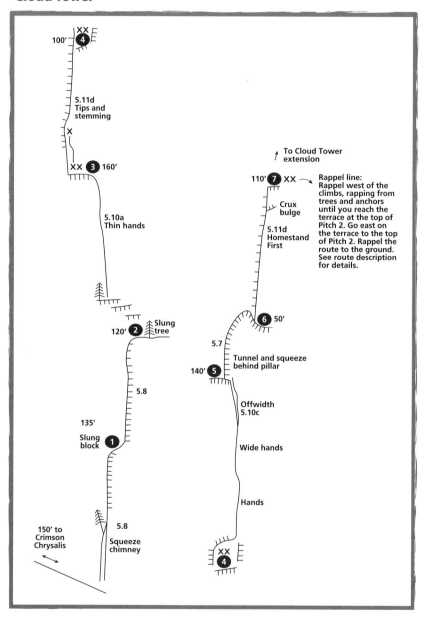

100' **4** XX

5.11d
Tips and stemming

X

XX **3** 160'

5.10a
Thin hands

120' **2** Slung tree

5.8

135'
Slung block **1**

150' to Crimson Chrysalis

5.8
Squeeze chimney

To Cloud Tower extension

110' **7** XX

Rappel line:
Rappel west of the climbs, rapping from trees and anchors until you reach the terrace at the top of Pitch 2. Go east on the terrace to the top of the route. Rappel the route to the ground. See route description for details.

Crux bulge

5.11d
Homestand First

6 50'

5.7

140' **5** Tunnel and squeeze behind pillar

Offwidth 5.10c

Wide hands

Hands

XX **4**

Crimson Chrysalis. The base of the route can be identified by a small chimney. A tree is growing out of the chimney/crack about 8 feet above the ground. **Pitch 1:** Worm up the squeeze chimney to the hand crack in the left-facing corner (5.8, 135 feet). **Pitch 2:** Continue up the corner to a ledge (5.8, 120 feet). **Pitch 3:** Traverse up and left, climbing over a few blocky ledges and passing a tree, to attain a beautiful hand crack. Work up the crack until it ends, then face climb left to the base of a right-facing corner (5.10a, 160 feet). **Pitch 4:** Crank up discontinuous cracks, past a bolt and into the corner. Follow the corner— tips and stemming—as it angles right to a belay in an alcove below a roof (5.11d, 100 feet). **Pitch 5:** Climb up to the roof, 10 feet above the anchor, and pull through it. The hand crack above widens throughout the remainder of the pitch (5.10c, 140 feet). **Pitch 6:** Climb up through a short wide section and then tunnel through the tower. It's a bit of a squeeze! Step down to a belay on a ledge (5.7, 50 feet). **Pitch 7:** Say hello to the sun and blast up the Indian Creek–style hand crack in a right-facing corner. The bulk of this pitch is 5.11a, but the final moves up the overhanging corner and over the little roof at the top are a solid 5.11c (5.11c, 110 feet). **Descent:** The rappel line drops down to the right (west) of the climb. You might be tempted to link rappels, but be aware that the area is known for rope-eating. Rappel 1: Make a 200-foot rappel from the top anchor to a tree approximately 30 feet below a big ledge. Rappel 2: Drop down from the tree to the base of a steep wall in a 150-foot rappel. Skip the anchor at the chockstone. Rappel 3: Make a 95-foot rappel to another tree on a ledge. Rappel 4: Make another shorter (90-foot) rappel to the top of pitch 2. Rappel 5: Rap 120 feet to the top of pitch 1. Rappel 6: Make a final 135-foot rappel to the ground. Pro: There are a lot of opinions on pro for this route, but the consensus for a full rack is a set of wires, doubles from 0.75 to 4 inches, triples of 0.4 and 0.5 inch, and five 2.5-inch pieces. **FA:** Paul Van Betten, Richard Harrison, and Nick Nordblom, 1983.

3. Cloud Tower Extension (5.12d) This extension takes climbers to the top of the tower. Approach via the first seven pitches of Cloud Tower. **Pitch 8:** Continue up, passing five bolts to a bolted anchor below an off-width (5.12d, 80 feet). **Pitch 9:** Climb the offwidth and squeeze chimney to the notch behind the Cloud Tower summit (5.10c, 100 feet). **Pitch 10:** Scramble up to the top of Crimson Chrysalis. **Descent:** Rappel Crimson Chrysalis. **FA:** Merlin Larsen and Dan McQuade, 2003.

GINGER BUTTRESS

The Ginger Buttress is a highly visible feature on the northeast flank of Rainbow Mountain. Ginger Cracks is one of the often-overlooked moderate classics of Red Rock, and Unimpeachable Groping is an incredibly cool, steep, and sporty route. The buttress doesn't see anywhere near the crowds of the nearby Cloud Tower.

Approach: From the Pine Creek parking area, drop down the main trail. A short time after leaving your car, the Fire Ecology Trail appears on the left. Take this trail and follow it across two washes toward the steep trail that cuts up the hillside. Climb up the steep trail to the top of the hill and follow the trail to a T junction with a sign that has an arrow on it. Go right on this trail. After a few minutes, you come to another junction. Take the right-hand fork down into the wash and back toward Pine Creek Canyon for a moment. After crossing the depression, take the first left-hand trail. Follow this trail across the major deep wash that comes out from between Rainbow Mountain and Jackrabbit Buttress. Cross the wash, then turn right on braided trails and work up the giant ramp to the obvious pink tower with the red top on the north end of Rainbow Mountain. At the base of the Cloud Tower approach ramp, cut left up the gully toward the base of the Ginger Buttress. **Time:** 1.5 hours.

Sun Exposure: Both routes on the Ginger Buttress see morning sun and afternoon shade.

Types of Climbing Available: Long multi-pitch trad and mixed climbing

1. Unimpeachable Groping (5.10b, IV, 800 feet, mixed/sport) A tribute to a scandal involving a former president and an intern, this line is essentially a sport route. A few pieces of gear may help to decrease some mild runouts, but a bold sport climber will have no problem climbing this line without additional protection. Approach by climbing up the gully next to the Ginger Buttress. This is the bolted line to the left of a large arching chimney system. The first pitch climbs up a combination of the rock face and a large pine tree approximately halfway up the gully. **Pitch 1:** Use a combination of your childhood tree climbing skills and your adult rock climbing skills to reach the first bolt. Continue past bolts up to a bolted station at a stance (5.10a, 120 feet). **Pitch 2:** Follow the bolt line up to an anchor (5.10b, 110 feet). **Pitch 3:** Continue up the bolted line to a bolted anchor on a large ledge (5.10a, 50 feet). Pitches 2 and 3 can easily be linked. **Pitch 4:** Pull through the roof and then continue up the face to the anchor (5.10b, 80 feet). **Pitch 5:** More steep climbing past more bolts leads to another anchor (5.10b, 80 feet). **Pitch 6:** Continue up 5.10 terrain, passing

Ginger Buttress

Power
Failure
Descent

1

2

more bolts. The climbing eases as you go. Belay at an anchor on a big ledge (5.10b, 80 feet). Pitch 5 and 6 may be linked. **Pitch 7:** Continue up into the lichen, but don't worry, the rock is good! Pass several more bolts to reach the top of the pillar (5.8, 160 feet). **Descent:** There are two descent options: You can rappel the route with double ropes from the top of pitch 6, or you can descend Power Failure. To descend Power Failure, rappel down into the bowl to the south. Scramble down a brushy trail to a bolted anchor at the top of Power Failure. Beware of loose rock here, as there may be parties below. Three double-rope rappels will bring you into the gully up and left of Unimpeachable Groping. Pro: Fifteen quickdraws. If you wish to bring gear to supplement protection, consider one 0.5-inch cam, two 0.75-inch cams, one 1-inch cam, and a handful of wires. **FA:** Mike Clifford and Jorge Urioste, 1999.

Micah Lewkowitz leads a stellar
pitch high on Ginger Cracks.

PHOTO BY JONATHON SPITZER

2. Ginger Cracks (5.9, IV, 955 feet, trad) This route is found just to the right of an arching chimney system on the prow of the buttress. Look for a wide 6-inch crack that works its way up to a tree. **Pitch 1:** Climb up the wide crack to a tree approximately 40 feet off the ground. Step right and climb the right-hand line in the double crack system. Move left and work up to a bolted belay station at the top of a flake (5.7, 110 feet). **Pitch 2:** Step down and right into a crack. Crank your way up through a short chimney and then up more thin cracks, passing a bolt to another bolted belay station (5.8, 150 feet). **Pitch 3:** Continue up the right-facing corner, passing a small roof. Climb up the wide crack to a double-bolt anchor (5.7+, 90 feet). **Pitch 4:** Step right to the crack on the right. Follow the crack up, passing two bolts to another bolted anchor (5.9, 150 feet). **Pitch 5:** Send the bulge above the anchor and then continue up the crack. Traverse left to a ledge and then work up to a tree for the belay (5.8, 175 feet). **Pitch 6:** Scramble up the bushy ledge system to a chimney. Climb up left and build an anchor at the base of a left-facing corner (5.0, 160 feet). **Pitch 7:** Climb up the left-facing corner and traverse to the right over a chimney. Continue up the main corner to the notch at the top of the buttress (5.6, 120 feet). **Descent:** Rappel down into the bowl to the south. Scramble down a brushy trail to a bolted anchor at the top of Power Failure. Beware of loose rock here, as there may be parties below. Three double-rope rappels will bring you into the gully up and left of Ginger Cracks. Pro to 3 inches. **FA:** Mark Moore and Lars Holbek, 1977.

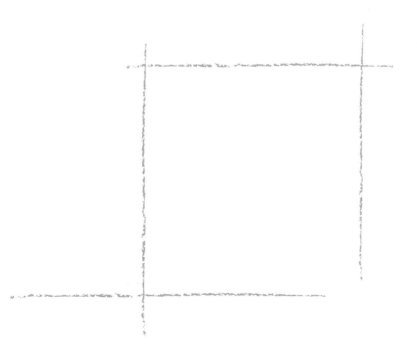

Oak Creek Canyon

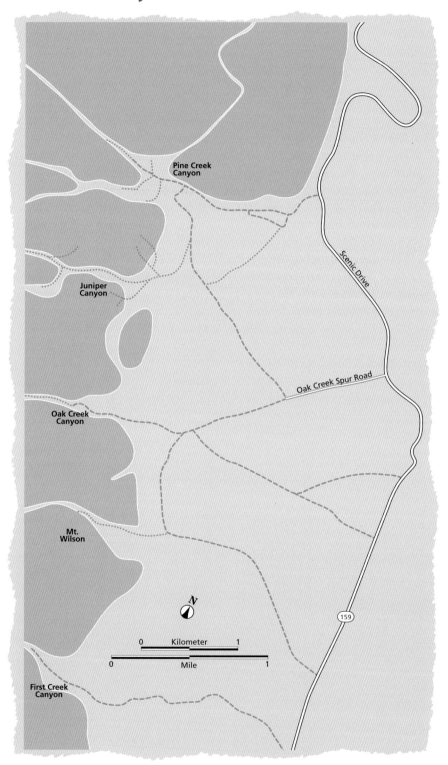

Pine Creek
Canyon

Scenic Drive

Oak Creek Spur Road

Juniper
Canyon

Oak Creek
Canyon

Mt.
Wilson

N

| 0 | Kilometer | 1 |
| 0 | Mile | 1 |

159

First Creek
Canyon

10.

Oak Creek Canyon

Oak Creek Canyon sports several beautiful long lines and lots of options for when there are a lot of people around. The area is particularly popular in the winter, as many of the routes are in the sun throughout the dark season.

Approach: There are two options for your approach. The first is to use the Red Rock Canyon Scenic Drive. To do this, drive 12.1 miles on the scenic drive to a dirt road on the right. Take this road for approximately a mile and park at the trailhead.

The second option is to park on NV 159, approximately half a mile from the scenic drive's exit. Though this trail is approximately 15 minutes longer, you can park on the road early in the morning to get an earlier start, and you don't have to spend time driving through the loop.

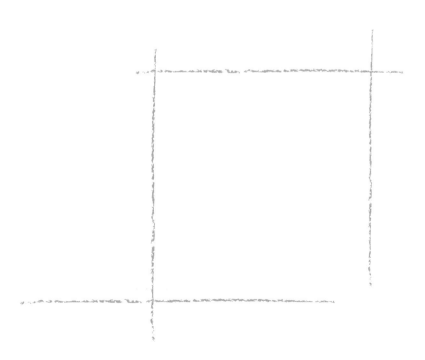

SOLAR SLAB WALL

The most popular route on the Solar Slab Wall is Solar Slab, a wonderful 5.6 romp. For most of this route's life, it didn't have bolted rappel stations, and it was common for climbers to spend the night high on the wall. Today, every station is bolted, and it's reasonable to rappel off when it starts to get late. That said, 5.6 climbers should plan for an early start and should understand that faster parties may wish to pass them.

The second most popular route in the area is Johnny Vegas, a shorter line that is also super fun. This route is commonly used as a means to access the upper Solar Slab Wall and often has a line early in the day.

Approach: Follow one of the two approach trails detailed in this chapter's introduction. After approximately 20 minutes of hiking, the trail gently curves to the right and then back to the left while descending a small hill (the first time the trail descends on the approach). Immediately after the curve, take the first spur trail to the right. Follow this somewhat broken and braided trail until directly beneath the Solar Slab area. A somewhat steep and loose trail on red

Solar Slab Wall

Photo by Andy Stephen

dirt switchbacks up through some jumbled rocks to the base of Solar Slab Gully. Johnny Vegas is just to the left and starts behind a boulder approximately 30 feet up. Beulah's Book starts to the left of that. The toe of Sunspot Ridge is far to the left and starts almost in the creek bed. **Time:** 45 minutes.

The Solar Slab Wall is broken into two major tiers. Beulah's Book, Johnny Vegas, and Solar Slab Gully are on the bottom tier, whereas Going Nuts, Arch Enemy, Solar Slab, and Sundog are on the upper tier.

Sun Exposure: The Solar Slab Wall is in the sun all day. However, the bottom of the wall goes into the shade in the winter for about an hour late in the morning.

Types of Climbing Available: Long, moderate multi-pitch crack and face climbs. One adventure climb!

1. Sunspot Ridge (5.8 R, IV, 1,500 feet, trad) This is an excellent adventure route in an awesome position. However, due to the fact that this line is seldom climbed, climbers should expect some route-finding challenges, difficult protection, loose rock, and some runouts. These challenges are well worth it, though. That's what adventure climbing is all about! The base of this route is found to the west of the lower tier of the Solar Slab Wall and climbs almost right out of the streambed. The ridge is essentially the line that separates the Solar Slab

Wall area from the Black Orpheus area. There are tons of variations, but the goal is to stay on the ridge up to the shelf above Solar Slab. Due to the nature of the route, the description here is slightly more vague. Use this as a template and follow your nose. It's been reported that this climb can be done in as few as seven pitches with a 70-meter rope, or as many as fourteen pitches. Do what makes sense to you. To attain the route, climb up through some brush to a gully system and an alcove on the left side of the southeast-facing buttress. Climb up a crack on the left and belay in a chimney. Move up right over a bulge and climb the varnished face. Move left and belay on a ledge. Climb up to a triangular roof, then cut right to a left-slanting crack. Continue up the crack to the Shoulder. From there, scramble up a 4th-class pitch to a belay near a bush. Launch out onto the face, straight up the ridge crest to a belay. Send another thin face pitch up the ridge to some decent ledges. Make two 4th-class pitches to "The Notch," the location where the ridge merges with the main wall. Blast up a 5.0 headwall above, climbing beautiful varnished rock. Make another 5.7 pitch up one of the two cracks to the top of the Solar Slab Wall. **Note:** It's recommended that you climb Solar Slab prior to making this ascent. It will give you a better idea on the descent. **Descent:** Rappel Solar Slab with double ropes (see the

Solar Slab description for details). Pro to 4 inches. Some have stated that ball nuts are desirable, but the author found the route to be fine without them. **FA:** John Hegyes, John Wilder, Jorge Urioste, and Larry DeAngelo.

2. Beulah's Book (5.9, II, 500 feet, trad) This is a cool route with lots of variety. The line is found approximately 100 feet left of Solar Slab Gully, left of Johnny Vegas. The first pitch can be identified by the dihedral start and the jammed block about 20 feet up. **Pitch 1:** Climb up a corner and then step left at the chockstone. Continue up the rib, passing a bolt, stopping at a belay ledge below

the chimney (5.7, 160 feet). **Pitch 2:** Continue up the chimney past a bolt and into the bomb bay. Before popping out like a cork, reach around the corner and attain the perfect jam crack. Jam up the crack and corner to a double-bolt belay on white rock (5.9, 150 feet). Variation 1: Climb up the arête left of the chimney to attain the same belay anchor, passing three bolts along the way (5.8+). Variation 2: If the chimney seems too difficult, but the dihedral corner above it seems more reasonable, it's also possible to climb up the arête for a short distance and then traverse right into the corner. Use long slings on the bolts to do this, or there will be a lot of drag

Solar Slab Wall

The lower tier of Solar Slab Wall

(5.9). **Pitch 3:** Continue up the white slab above. There is limited protection here, so take it where you can get it. Climb up a short, steep section, then continue up and right on easier terrain to some left-leaning cracks and build an anchor (5.5, 150 feet). **Pitch 4:** Scramble up easy terrain to the Solar Slab ledge (5.0, 60 feet). **Descent:** Rappel Solar Slab Gully (see specific descent information in the Solar Slab Gully route description). Pro to 4 inches. **FA:** Randal Grandstaff and Dave Anderson, 1979.

3. Johnny Vegas (5.7, II, 630 feet, trad) This route lies to the left of the Solar Slab Gully. It may be identified by the crack system working its way up behind a boulder approximately 30 feet off the ground. The end of the first pitch is quite visible from the base as the crack system reaches a right-facing corner. **Pitch 1:** Make a short lead up the corner system behind a tree and a large block. Stop behind the large boulder and reconfigure for the first real pitch (5.5, 40 feet). Variation: The first pitch can be bypassed in a right-facing corner system to the left. **Pitch 2:** Follow the left-trending cracks up to a double-bolt belay (5.6, 140 feet). Variation: The first two pitches can be bypassed in a right-facing corner system to the left (5.7+, 140 feet). **Pitch 3:** Continue up the wide corner and out onto the face. Gear on this pitch becomes somewhat sparse near the top. Climb up to a double-bolt anchor (5.7, 130 feet). **Pitch 4:** Climb up to the right. Protection is sparse, so protect when feasible. Note that it is possible to thread a sling through a hole just up and right of the anchor for a piece. Continue up until a crack system shoots out to the left above a small roof. Use long slings here to avoid drag. Follow these cracks up and left to a double-bolt anchor (5.6, 130 feet). Variation: There is a crack system on the left-hand side of the anchor that leads up to a bolt. This variation requires 5.9 slab climbing just before the bolt (5.9, 130 feet). **Pitch 5:** Climb straight up the face to a ledge with large boulders on it and build a belay (5.0, 50 feet). **Pitch 6:** The top of pitch 5 is the traditional end of Johnny Vegas. However, to attain the large ledge below Solar Slab, scramble up 3rd- and 4th-class terrain behind the boulders to the massive vegetated ledge (4th class, 300 feet). **Descent:** It is possible to rappel Johnny Vegas with double ropes, but it is not advisable. Johnny Vegas is a notorious rope-eater. Instead, descend Solar Slab Gully (see specific descent information in the Solar Slab Gully route description). Pro to 4 inches. **FA:** Harrison Shull, Tom Cecil, Dave Cox, and Todd Hewitt, 1994.

4. Solar Slab Gully (5.5, II-, 500 feet, trad) This is a nice beginner multipitch. However, you should be aware that this gully drains the entire south face of Rainbow Mountain following a storm. If there is snow high on the mountain, the gully often gets wet in the afternoon as the snow melts. **Pitch 1:** Follow the central crack system. Approximately 60 feet up there is a small ledge with a double-bolt anchor on the left-hand side. It is possible to build a belay here. Most parties elect to continue climbing for another 70 feet to a ledge with a tree. A second set of bolt anchors is found here (5.3, 140 feet). **Pitch 2:** Before climbing the second pitch, move the belay 30 feet up the gully behind the second tree directly beneath the start of the second pitch. Climb past a single crux move up and left to belay at a set of bolts (5.3, 50 feet). **Pitch 3:** Before ascending the third pitch, move the belay over to the sandy ledge with a large rock in the center. Climb up to the right into a small chimney. Pull out of the chimney and continue up along a right-facing corner toward a steep wall. Cut to the left up the line of weakness at the break in the right-facing corner. Continue up and right to a large ledge. Scramble/walk past the bolts to a tree approximately 30 feet back and belay there (5.3, 160 feet). **Pitch 4:** Move the belay up the gully to the base of a short, steep section that is frequently wet—often referred to as the "Waterfall Pitch." Chimney and stem up slightly overhung terrain to a pair of bolts (5.5, 25 feet). **Pitch 5:** Move the belay up to a flat spot near the last bush and then climb up the easy, but often wet, gully to the top of the route. Step up and left and belay off trees or natural gear. There are bolts on the right, but it's a harder spot to manage a belay (5.3, 30 feet).

Descent: It is possible to descend this route with a single 60-meter rope. Locate a pair of bolts on the right (east) side of the gully. Rappel 1: Make a 25-foot rappel to the top of the Waterfall Pitch. Rappel 2: Make a second 25-foot rappel to the bottom of the Waterfall Pitch. It's possible to link these rappels, but ropes often get stuck. Walk down to the bolts at the top of pitch 3 (skier's left). Rappel 3: Rappel 80 feet to a slung pillar midway up Pitch 3. Rappel 4: Rappel 80 feet to the sandy ledge. Scramble 20 feet down the gully to a pair of bolts at the top of Pitch 2. Rappel 5: Rappel 50 feet to the top of pitch 1. Rappel 6: Rappel 60 feet from these bolts to a ledge with a bolted anchor. Rappel 7: Make one more 80-foot rappel to the ground. Pro to 3 inches. **FA:** Unknown.

5. Going Nuts (5.6, III-, 820 feet, trad) This very cool route is found on the second tier, above Johnny Vegas and Solar Slab Gully. The line starts in a corner/groove system to the left of the giant arch. **Pitch 1:** Start in the groove on the left side of the Solar Slab Wall. Climb the groove, working into the right-hand crack. As the crack begins to peter out, move up and left onto a small stance in the

Solar Slab Wall

Tunnel through or behind

Build Anchor with Nuts

Top of Pitch 2

8

5

6

7

The upper tier of Solar Slab Wall

broken patina. Build an anchor out of wired nuts (5.6, 170 feet). **Pitch 2:** Launch up and left, climbing through the patina. Beware of loose rock. Work up to the ledge on the left-hand side of the giant arch and build a gear anchor. **Descent:** Work climber's right across the top of the arch toward Solar Slab. A belay may be required to move across exposed terrain while passing the bushes. Once across the arch, drop down and left to the rappel anchors at the top of pitch 3 of Solar Slab. Make a 150-foot double-rope rappel, passing a set of bolts on a ledge near the Arch Enemy squeeze hole, and continue down to a ledge with a tree and bolts. Make a second double-rope rappel (160 feet) to the big ledge. Rappel Solar Slab Gully to reach the ground. Pro to 3 inches, with lots of wires. **FA:** Unknown.

6. Arch Enemy (5.10a, III-, 750 feet, trad) This wicked little route is found under the arch on the second tier of the Solar Slab Wall. Arch Enemy climbs up the right-hand crack beneath the arch and then tunnels through to join Solar Slab. **Pitch 1:** Climb up the slab near a black water streak, heading for the right-hand side of the arch. Protection is sparse, so get it when you can. Work up into the corner with more protection and build a belay at the double-bolt anchor (5.8, 160 feet). **Pitch 2:** Continue up the corner, passing two protection bolts until you can squeeze through the tunnel at the arch. Build a belay at the bolts in the corner (5.10a, 100 feet). **Descent:** Either continue up, or rappel Solar Slab with double ropes. **FA:** Unknown.

7. Solar Slab (5.6, III, 1,500 feet, trad) Found almost directly above Solar Slab Gully on the second tier of the Solar Slab Wall, this is a super-classic route at a beginner grade!

Many parties are benighted on this route. Some even unintentionally spend the night. If you are new to big multi-pitch climbs, be sure to bring a headlamp and consider a turnaround time. In October and November, those new to bigger multi-pitch routes should consider a 3 p.m. turnaround time; in December, January, and February, consider 2 p.m.; and in March, 3 p.m. Throughout the rest of the year, those new to biggish multi-pitch climbs should start to rappel at 4 p.m. to avoid getting stuck in the dark.

Pitch 1: Climb slabs up to a series of cracks in the face. The left crack is easier. Belay at a bolted anchor (5.6, 160 feet). **Pitch 2:** Ascend the corner to the top of the arch. Look down the squeeze chimney and then pass a double-bolt anchor. Continue up the right-facing corner to another double-bolt anchor (5.6, 150 feet). **Pitch 3:** There are two crack systems above. The left-hand crack is 5.6 and

the right-hand is 5.9. Follow intermittent cracks up to a double-bolt chain anchor. Clip this anchor and continue climbing up the left-hand side of the mushroom-shaped feature. Belay at the top of this feature at a bolted anchor (5.6, 150 feet). **Pitch 4:** Follow the crack system straight up from the belay. Once again you will pass a double-bolt anchor. Continue climbing until a small ledge is reached with a mildly larger one directly above it. This is the first break where it is possible to stop without hanging. Build an anchor here (5.6, 190 feet). **Pitch 5:** Continue straight up as the terrain eases. Follow cracks up to a double-bolt anchor (5.5, 160 feet). **Pitch 6:** Scramble up easy terrain to the ledge with boulders and small trees. Many people end their climb here because the descent from the top two pitches is exposed (4th class, 50 feet). **Pitch 7:** Scramble up to a corner and build a belay (4th class, 60 feet). **Pitch 8:** Climb the corner to the top of the wall (5.5, 70 feet). **Descent:** To get to the top of pitch 6, first work down to a bush. Then downclimb skier's left of the bush and scramble back down to the big ledge. From the top of pitch 6, scramble to the bolts at the top of pitch 5. Rappel 1: Make a double-rope rappel (150 feet) straight down to a set of anchors that were not visible on the way up, but that are approximately 20 feet to climber's right of the top of pitch 4. Rappel 2: Make a second 150-foot rappel to the anchor on top of the mushroom feature at the top of the third pitch. Rappel 3: Rappel 150 straight down to a hanging rappel station, or rappel 150 feet back to the top of pitch 2. Rappel 4: Rappel 150 feet to the bolts atop pitch 1. Rappel 5: Rappel 160 feet to the large ledge. Continue rappelling down Solar Slab Gully. Pro to 4 inches. **FA:** Joe Herbst, Tom Kaufmann, and Larry Hamilton, 1975.

8. Sundog (5.9+, III+, 1,270 feet, trad) This pleasant line climbs the right-hand side of the upper tier of the Solar Slab Wall. From the top of the Solar Slab Gully, scramble 200 feet right across slabs to a large bushy terrace. Sundog climbs the left-most groove above the terrace on the left-hand side of the bushy dirt area off the slabs. **Pitch 1:** Climb up the groove and into the corner to a single-bolt belay station, passing another bolt along the way. This is a thin pitch, so take protection where it presents itself (5.7, 190 feet). Variation: It is possible to avoid this pitch by scrambling around to the right. **Pitch 2:** Climb up the left-facing corner to a bolted stance (5.7, 100 feet). **Pitch 3:** Climb up through two bulges, passing four bolts to cracks. Continue up to another bolted stance (5.8, 165 feet). **Pitch 4:** Continue up the face, passing eight bolts to a crack. Work up to another bolted anchor (5.9, 150 feet). **Pitch 5:** Follow the right-facing corner to a wide crack. Make a few offwidth moves to easier terrain and a bolted anchor (5.9+). **Descent:** It's possible to scramble up and rappel Solar Slab. Conversely, it's also possible to rappel this line with double ropes. Rappel down to the top of the second pitch and then scramble down to skier's left. Pro to 4 inches. **FA:** Ed Prochaska and Joanne Urioste, 1997.

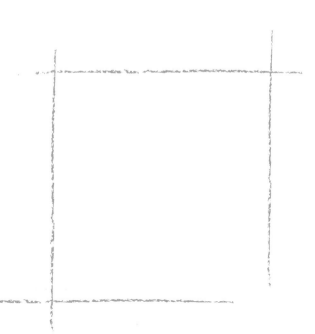

BLACK ORPHEUS AREA

This area is defined by a massive system of dihedrals just beyond the Sunspot Ridge. Black Orpheus—the featured line on the wall—links these corners together at a mostly moderate grade with a few harder moves here and there.

Jorge and Joanne Urioste put up Black Orpheus in 1979 in a single push. Historically, they used fixed lines to attack big features. But on this first ascent they went old school. The result was that they were forced to endure a bivy high on the mountain, something that still occasionally happens today.

The pair named their classic route after a 1959 movie that modernized another classic. *Black Orpheus* tells the tragic Greek story of the doomed love between Orpheus and Eurydice. After Eurydice dies, Orpheus must descend into the underworld to find her.

Black Orpheus, the route, is no descent into the underworld. Instead, many consider it an ascent into the heavens! Personally, I just think the route is wickedly cool!

Approach: Follow one of the two approach trails detailed in this chapter's introduction. After approximately 20 minutes of hiking, the trail gently curves to the right and then back to the left while descending a small hill (the first time the trail descends on the approach). Immediately after the curve, take the first spur trail to the right. Follow this somewhat broken and braided trail until directly beneath the Solar Slab area. Continue to follow the trail as it drops down into the streambed. Pass beneath the toe of the Sunspot Ridge and continue. Climb up out of the creek bed approximately 300 yards beyond the toe of Sunspot Ridge, then turn right and scramble directly up 500 feet of 3rd class with an occasional 4th-class move to the toe of a giant left-facing corner. It's best to carry your gear over this route. **Time:** 1.5 hours.

Sun Exposure: The bottom of Black Orpheus is in the shade in the morning, but the bulk of the route is in the sun all day.

Types of Climbing Available: Mostly moderate multi-pitch adventure climbing on a big and cool feature

1. Black Orpheus (5.10a R, IV, 1,300 feet, trad) The profile of Black Orpheus starts with a large left-facing corner system for three pitches. The route moves leftward across easier terrain for a handful of pitches and then finishes primarily in the giant right-facing corner. **Pitch 1:** Climb up the left-facing corner to a double-bolt anchor (5.8, 110 feet). **Pitch 2:** Climb up the corner to a ledge. Make a few awkward lieback moves to attain a second bolted anchor (5.8, 140 feet). **Pitch 3:** Step up to a bolt and then back into the corner. Belay on a big ledge (5.7, 110 feet). **Note:** The goal of the next four pitches is to attain

PHOTO BY LARRY DEANGELO

Black Orpheus

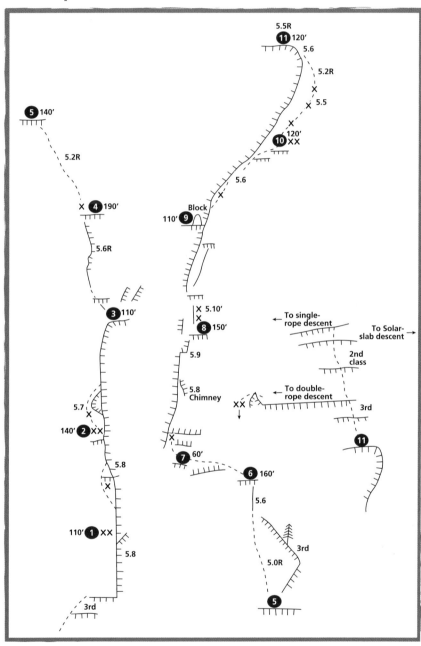

the giant left-facing corner above and left. **Pitch 4:** Move up left, climbing through a runout 5.6 lieback. Climb up a left-leaning crack to a ledge with one bolt. Supplement the bolt with a wire and belay (5.6 R, 190 feet). **Pitch 5:** Continue up and left on the runout ramp to a ledge (5.2 R, 140 feet). **Pitch 6:** There are two options to start this pitch: First, it's possible to go straight up on runout 5.0 terrain; or second, it's also possible to move up and right, passing a tree on 3rd-class terrain. These two options come together at a 5.6 crack. Follow this left and then make some face moves to attain a stance below an overhang (5.6, 160 feet). **Pitch 7:** Traverse left to the base of a right-facing dihedral (5.0, 60 feet). **Pitch 8:** Make a few exciting face moves up left, passing a bolt and into the corner. Jam and chimney your way up some phenomenal climbing, finishing the pitch with a funky move up and right to a ledge and the belay (5.9, 150 feet). **Pitch 9:** Make the crux finger jam moves and then continue up, passing two bolts into the corner. Follow twin cracks up to a series of ledges. Belay on the higher of the two ledges (5.10a, 110 feet). **Pitch 10:** Work up the 5.6 corner, passing a bolt. As the climbing eases, step right to a double-bolt anchor (5.6, 120 feet). **Pitch 11:** Arc out right, passing three bolts. Skip the fourth bolt on the left, as it's old and off-route. Continue up the runout face and back to the corner. Follow the crack to the top (5.6, 120 feet). **Pitch 12:** Scramble to the top, stopping on a ledge above a little arch. **Descent:** There are three common options to descend. Option 1—Double-Rope **Descent:** From the top of pitch 11, scramble up to a big ledge. Traverse left (west) to a flake near where the ledge system begins to descend. Drop down behind the flake to an anchor. Make a 165-foot rappel to another anchor. Make a second 170-foot rappel to 3rd-class slabs. Drop down these slabs, working west until you reach a ledge. Drop down and left on 2nd- and 3rd-class terrain, working toward the wash. Option 2—Single-Rope **Descent:** Scramble to the top of the wall near the little arch. Move left to a ramp that drops down to a rappel anchor. Make an 80-foot rappel to a large ledge and then walk west for approximately 150 feet. Make a second 80-foot rappel down a chimney to a ledge. Scramble down and left to another anchor and make a third 80-foot rappel. From there, drop down white slabs toward a large bench with a big boulder on it, known as the IBM boulder. Go right (west) and make your way down a ramp system to the creek bed. Option 3—Rappel Solar Slab: If you are familiar with the very top of Solar Slab and can find the rappels, this is an excellent double-rope-rappel way down. If you are not familiar with the top of the feature, one of the other two options is better. Pro to 4 inches. **FA:** Jorge and Joanne Urioste, 1979.

EAGLE WALL

The Eagle Wall is a climber's dream. The wall is big, featured, and beautiful. From a distance the central portion of the cliff face appears to be blank. Indeed, it is not blank. There are fantastic lines hidden in the texture of the rock.

The wall was initially named after the image of an eagle that appears to some in the varnish halfway up the wall. Personally, I don't see it. Perhaps, like the image of a saint on a piece of toast, it only appears to the worthy!

Approach: Follow one of the two approach trails detailed in this chapter's introduction. After approximately 20 minutes of hiking, the trail gently curves to the right and then back to the left while descending a small hill (the first time the trail descends on the approach). Immediately after the curve, take the first spur trail to the right. Follow this somewhat broken and braided trail until directly beneath the Solar Slab area. Continue to follow the trail as it drops down into the streambed. Pass beneath the toe of the Sunspot Ridge and continue. Follow the creek bed to the fork and take the right-hand (north) fork. Follow this for 15 minutes. Look for two massive pine trees in the center of the drainage. Head up slabs from the right-hand tree, following the path of least resistance toward the

Eagle Wall

Eagle Wall approaches
PHOTO BY ANDREW YASSO

Eagle Wall

Painted Bowl

Giant Pine Trees

IBM Boulder

feature. Climb through a gully, drop down, and then work back up to the base of the wall. **Time:** 2 hours.

A second, slightly faster approach requires a little better knowledge of the area. Prior to arriving at the two pine trees, cut up slabs toward the IBM boulder. From there, scramble up toward the base of the Rainbow Buttress on the right-hand side of the Eagle Wall. Expect some 4th-class scrambling. **Time:** 1.5 hours.

Sun Exposure: The Eagle Wall is in the sun all day.

Types of Climbing Available: Advanced-level mixed multi-pitch climbing; classic moderate multi-pitch trad climbing

1. Eagle Dance (5.10c A0, IV+, 1,000 feet, mixed) The base of Eagle Dance is found 50 feet right of a pillar in a small black corner and 50 feet left of Levitation 29. **Pitch 1:** Climb up the dihedral to a ledge (5.9, 90 feet). **Pitch 2:** Continue to follow the same crack system (5.8, 120 feet). **Pitch 3:** Use long slings at the start of this pitch to avoid drag. Step up and right, working into a seam and passing six bolts. Look for an anchor on the right; continue past this, clipping four more bolts to attain an anchor next to a cave (5.10a, 160 feet). **Pitch 4:** Clip a long sling to the first bolt and then climb past fourteen bolts, passing through the "eagle's neck"

Eagle Wall

PHOTO BY ANDREW YASSO

Eagle Wall

Upper Painted Bowl

to the next anchor (5.10c, 90 feet). **Pitch 5:** Follow the trail of nine bolts to an anchor (5.10a, 120 feet). **Pitch 6:** Crank up through a 5.9 move to a bolt. Step right onto a ramp and make a few moves until it's possible to attain the right-facing corner. Beware of loose flakes here. Continue up the corner, clipping two bolts before attaining the anchor (5.10a, 50 feet). Many people bail from here, but it's well worth finishing the route. **Pitch 7:** Follow a 5.9 crack to the left. Aid through the technical terrain on eight bolts (5.9 A0, 60 feet). **Pitch 8:** Make a short pitch up the left-facing corner, passing four bolts to an anchor. This pitch is awkward on soft rock (5.10a, 40 feet). **Pitch 9:** Continue up the very awkward corner, passing seven bolts to attain an anchor on a big ledge. This is the crux pitch. It is possible to rappel from here, but it is not possible to rappel from any higher, as there are no more fixed anchors (5.10c, 100 feet). **Pitch 10:** The left-facing corner continues, albeit less steeply, past four more bolts (5.9, 130 feet). **Pitch 11:** Scramble to the top (5.0, 100 feet). **Descent:** It is possible to rappel the route from the top of pitch 10 with double ropes. Note that it is not possible to rappel from Pitch 7 to the top of pitch 6. Instead, rappel to the top of pitch 5. Continue rapping from there to the ground. Alternatively, if you choose to climb to the top, walk off to the west. Make your way toward the red tower (George Washington Tower)

and scramble past it on the right side of the feature. Continue west to the other side of the tower and onto the ridge. Follow this to the gully systems that drop down south and into the upper reaches of Oak Creek Canyon. Expect it to take 2-plus hours to get from the top of the feature back to your car.

2. Levitation 29 (5.11c, IV+, 1,000 feet, mixed) Lynn Hill considers this to be one of the best climbs she's ever done. That's no small compliment coming from the woman who became the first person to ever free the Nose on El Capitan! The base of this route is found 150 feet to the right of Eagle Dance at a series of varnished cracks. **Pitch 1:** Climb up past two bolts to varnished cracks. Continue up through the cracks to two more bolts and a bolted anchor (5.10a, 80 feet). **Pitch 2:** Step up and right and climb through a series of steep flakes, passing eight bolts to an anchor. **Pitch 3:** Follow a left-trending crack system, then step right and clip two bolts. Scamper up to the anchor (5.8, 120 feet). **Pitch 4:** Climb past a roof and onto the face, clipping seven bolts as you go. If you intend to rappel the route, it is possible to leave the second rope here to decrease weight for the remainder of the climb (5.10b, 140 feet). **Pitch 5:** Move up from the belay to a steep and pumpy crack and corner system. Clip thirteen bolts before reaching the next bolted

Eagle Wall

A foreshortened image of the Eagle Wall. The bottom pitches are not visible in this photo.
PHOTO BY MIKE LAYTON

anchor (5.11c, 90 feet). **Pitch 6:** Continue to work up the crack system, arcing slowly to the left and passing five bolts (5.10d, 60 feet). **Pitch 7:** Climb up the face to a scoop and then work right into a bolted corner to the anchor. This pitch has thirteen bolts on it. Many people choose to rappel after this pitch (5.11a, 85 feet). **Pitch 8:** Climb up the left side of a flake to a bolt. Work up to the top to another bolt and then traverse approximately 20 feet right to a crack. Follow this crack as it slants up and left. Eventually you will reach a line of five more bolts. Once you've clipped the fifth, traverse left to the anchor on a slab (5.10a, 90 feet). **Pitch 9:** Step left off the anchor, avoiding the loose block. Follow seven bolts up to an anchor below a ledge with a tree on it (5.9, 90 feet). **Pitch 10:** Climb up to the tree at the top (5.6, 40 feet). **Descent:** It is possible to rappel the route with double ropes. It is also possible to walk off via the Eagle Dance walk-off descent. Pro to 2 inches. Most people only carry a single rack. **FA:** Bill Bradley and Jorge and Joanne Urioste, 1981. **FFA:** Lynn Hill, John Long, and Joanne Urioste, 1981.

3. Rainbow Buttress (5.8+ R, IV+, 1,000 feet, trad) This is a big route, and many of those whose leading abilities top out at 5.8 will find it challenging to climb this route and get back to the car with daylight to spare. The approach is long, there are no bolted anchors on the route, and the descent is longer. All of this should be taken into account prior to approaching this line. Strategize and be successful! The Rainbow Buttress is found

Rainbow Buttress

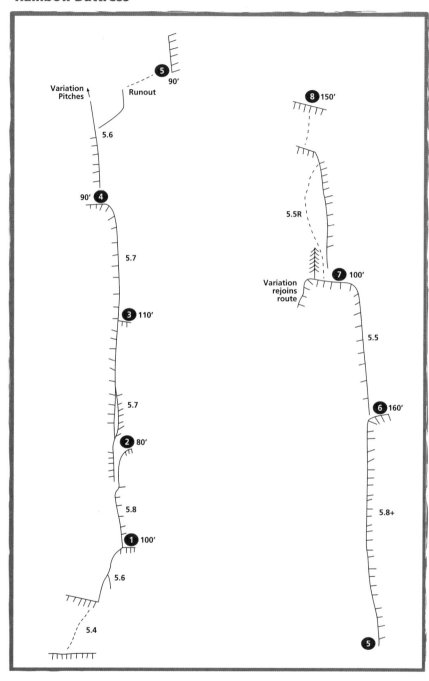

on the right side of the Rainbow Wall, and the route starts at the top of the approach ramp at a notch where you can look down into the Painted Bowl. **Pitch 1:** Launch up from the notch. Climb right on the face to a dihedral. Work up to a belay ledge (5.6, 100 feet). **Pitch 2:** Climb up past a roof and into the left-facing corner. Continue up this to another ledge (5.8, 80 feet). **Pitch 3:** Do battle with the offwidth, then move out on the face for a few moves. Step back into the corner and climb up the easier crack to a belay ledge approximately 20 feet below a bush (5.7, 110 feet). **Pitch 4:** Continue up the corner into a chimney and then finally to the top of the Black Tower (5.7, 90 feet). **Pitch 5:** Climb up from the top of the Black Tower for approximately 40 feet, until it is possible to traverse right on the face. This 40-foot traverse is a bit runout. Build an anchor with large gear at the base of the large left-facing corner (5.6, 90 feet). This brings you to the base of the Dihedral Variation.

Variation: The original line climbed the left-hand side of the Black Tower. These days most people do the traverse. But the original line is fun too. It essentially makes three 5.8ish pitches to the top of the tower. They follow the left side of the feature and the left-facing corner. Once at the top you can rejoin the "Dihedral Variation" at the bottom of pitch 8. The three left-side pitches are broken into the following: 5.8, 90 feet; 5.7, 75 feet; and 5.7, 195 feet. **Pitch 6:** From the base of the dihedral, climb up this crux pitch using a combination of fist jams and stems. Build a belay on a large ledge (5.8+, 160 feet). **Pitch 7:** Climb up the low-angle crack and chimney system to a large sloping ledge with a tree on it (5.5, 100 feet). **Pitch 8:** Climb up the sandy face left of the left-facing corner. Work up to a wide crack system and continue up to the top. This is a very runout pitch (5.5, 150 feet). **Descent:** Walk off as per Eagle Dance. Pro to 4 inches. **FA:** Joe Herbst and Joe Frani, 1975.

Justin Thibault, Jay Hack, and the author at a bivy high on the Resolution Arête
PHOTO BY MIKE LAYTON

11.

Mount Wilson

Mount Wilson is a centerpiece of Red Rock climbing. The feature is a true mountain with many buttresses, walls, and summits. When the early morning sun paints the mountains with its rays, it's hard to imagine a more beautiful piece of rock.

Mount Wilson is known specifically for the fact that it harbors some of the longest and most complex climbs in the canyon. The two routes featured here are both Grade V climbs if an individual elects to climb to the summit, making high-mountain bivies common. This in itself is a special treat. The lights of Las Vegas from a ledge high on Mount Wilson are truly something to behold.

These routes to the summit are very serious endeavors, the Resolution Arête more so than Inti Watana. There is no water anywhere on them. And more than one strong party—even sponsored climbing athletes—have tried to complete one of these routes to the summit in a day only to find themselves lost somewhere high on the mountain and stuck at a forced bivy.

The Resolution Arête requires you to move effectively up the mountain. There are limited options for retreat without surrendering a large portion of your rack. Inti Watana has bolted anchors and is less serious. It is much easier to move fast on that route. If you're going to try to climb the mountain to the summit and back out to the car in a day, it's recommended that you try this less severe route first.

Approach: Park at the Old Oak Creek Campground, 1.4 miles south of the exit to the Red Rock Canyon Scenic Drive on NV 159. Follow the trail northwest to the Wilson Pimple. The trail begins to trend more directly west at that point. Continue to follow the trail for approximately 1.5 miles until a spur trail cuts off to the left toward the mountain and the Resolution Arête. Follow the spur up toward the deepest gully. Pass the first gully you come to and take the second. Follow this deep gully—which usually contains cairns—up under a chockstone. Expect 3rd-, 4th-, and maybe even a 5th-class move here or there in this gully approach. Eventually you will reach a large pine tree at the base of the wall. The Resolution Arête starts to the left of the pine tree. Another gully is visible to the right of the tree. Follow this gully up, tunneling through another chockstone, to find the base of Inti Watana. **Time:** 2 hours.

Sun Exposure: Both routes see morning sun, but fall into the shade in the afternoon. The bottom pitches of both routes are also in the shade early in the morning.

Types of Climbing Available: Big-ass adventure climbs

1. Resolution Arête (5.10d C1, or 5.11d, V, 2,500 feet, trad) This is one of the big boys of Red Rock. Commonly referred to as "The Rez" by locals, this line climbs the obvious skyline arête that stands out dramatically on the east face of Mount Wilson. It is especially visible from the Solar Slab area, as well as from Spring Mountain Ranch. The bottom part of the arête is composed of a massive triangular form. The line then climbs up a rib to the right of the enormous scoop on the east face of Mount Wilson and finally reaches the summit. It is a fantastic adventure climb. **Pitch 1:** The base of the route is 40 feet left of the ponderosa pine. Climb left into the right-facing corner and up through a small roof, and build a belay at a bolt (5.9, 100 feet). **Pitch 2:** Follow a crack up to the top of the red pillar (5.8, 150 feet). **Pitch 3:** Climb up the face to the right of the pillar to reach a right-facing corner. Continue up to belay at the base of a chimney. The protection on this pitch is a bit tricky (5.9, 140 feet). **Pitch 4:** Climb the chimney.

Mt. Wilson

Mount Wilson
PHOTO BY MIKE LAYTON

Resolution Arête

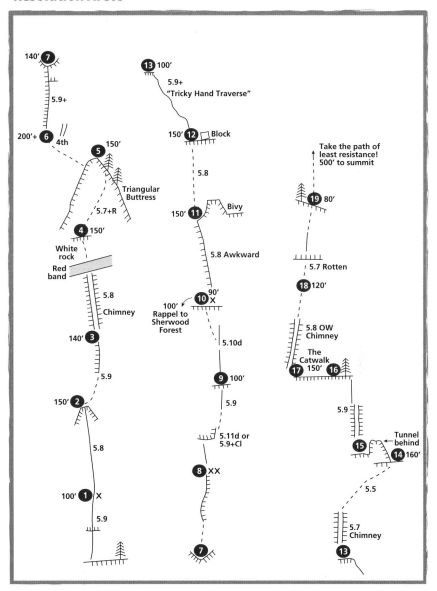

Climb through a red band to the highest ledge in the white rock (5.8, 150 feet). **Pitch 5:** Aim for the top and just right of the triangular buttress. Climb the face, trending right, up and toward large pine trees (5.7+ R, 150 feet). **Pitch 6:** Climb or simul left, through the notch and behind the buttress. Note that this is where the giant triangular tower leans against the upper arête. Work across, passing two cracks, to the base of a right-facing corner and build a belay. Beware of loose blocks (4th class, 200+ feet). **Pitch 7:** Climb up past the loose blocks and into the excellent right-facing corner. Build a belay in the alcove (5.9+, 140 feet). **Pitch 8:** Climb up the face and crack up to a belay 20 feet below a large roof (5.9, 100 feet). **Pitch 9:** Climb up to the roof and then make it happen. Either make a few aid moves, or crank through using the finger crack. There is some fixed gear here. Pull around the corner and continue up the 5.9+ face for 50 feet to a belay stance at the bottom of a thin left-facing corner. Some people free this pitch, some aid it, and others French-free it (5.11d or 5.9+ C1, 100 feet). **Pitch 10:** Climb up the corner, trending left to a ledge with a single bolt (5.10d, 90 feet). **Note:** Historically, people have made a 100-foot rappel down from here to Sherwood Forest (a vegetated area in the giant east-facing scoop) and a more comfortable bivy. Most modern climbers are able to get past this point on Day 1 to one of several other bivy options higher. **Pitch 11:** Climb up the left-leaning corner/ramp to a notch. There is another bivy option here through the notch and to the right (5.8, 150 feet). **Pitch 12:** Climb up steeply to easier terrain above. Continue up to a ledge with a block on it. A left-leaning crack is on the left side (5.8, 150 feet). **Pitch 13:** If this pitch were on the ground, it would get climbed daily. It's often referred to as "the tricky hand traverse." Climb up the left-leaning crack to a belay at the base of a chimney (5.9+, 100 feet). **Pitch 14:** Send the chimney to easier climbing on the face. Work up and right to the bottom of a pillar. Belay on the right-hand side in a recess. Use long slings to avoid drag (5.7, 160 feet). **Pitch 15:** Climb up into a tunnel on the pillar's right side and wiggle through to the base of a chimney. Build a belay (4th class, 80 feet). **Pitch 16:** Continue up the chimney. Step left as the difficulty increases. Make a 5.9 move to the left and then climb up to a crack. Follow this to a big ledge with a tree. Use long slings to avoid drag (5.9, 150 feet). **Pitch 17:** Walk left on the ledge to a chimney. This ledge is called "The Catwalk" (120 feet). **Pitch 18:** Climb up the left side of the chimney. Belay below a rotten white roof (5.8, 120 feet). **Pitch 19:** Climb up through the junky roof (be careful!) and continue up to a big

Inti Watana and the top of the Resolution Arête

PHOTO BY MIKE LAYTON

sloping ledge with a ponderosa pine (5.7, 80 feet). **Pitches 20–23:** Take the path of least resistance to the summit (4th class, 500 feet). **Descent:** Walk west toward the limestone for approximately half a mile. Do not drop down too early; if you do, you're going to epic. Eventually you will reach a big red pillar with what looks like a Volkswagen van carved out of rock on the top. Drop down the left-hand gully and start to scramble. There are two rappels in this gully. If you go down the wrong gully, there will be more. Continue down 3rd- and 4th-class terrain until you reach the South Fork of Oak Creek. Walk down the creek and ultimately out and back to your car (3-plus hours for the descent). Pro to 4 inches. Some people bring light aid gear; others are able to A0 or free climb through the crux. **FA:** Geoffrey Conley and Phil Broscovak, 1981. **FFA:** Paul Van Betten and Richard Harrison, 1984.

2. Inti Watana (5.10c, IV–V, 1,500 feet, mixed) While still big, this route doesn't have the level of commitment as the Resolution Arête. And, due to the fact that it is heavily bolted, you can climb the line much faster. Most people rappel at the end of pitch 12, keeping the route a Grade IV, but Inti Watana can also be combined with the upper pitches of the Resolution Arête, bisecting that route at pitch 14. However you choose to do it, this is a fun and engaging route. From the

pine tree to the right of the base of the Resolution Arête, look for another gully to the right. Climb up this gully and tunnel through a chockstone to the base of Inti Watana. Look for bolts to identify the start of the route. **Pitch 1:** Climb up the bolted face, passing seven bolts to an anchor (5.9+, 90 feet). **Pitch 2:** Climb up the steep headwall, passing ten bolts to a bolted belay stance (5.10c, 100 feet). **Pitch 3:** Continue up, working first to the right and then back to the left to a bolted anchor station (5.8, 140 feet). **Pitch 4:** Climb up the face to attain a series of thin cracks. Pass three bolts to attain the anchor in an alcove (5.9, 140 feet). **Pitch 5:** Step up and right to the first of two hand cracks. Follow the crack to its end. Step right again to a second crack and follow this up to a double-bolt belay (5.7, 130 feet). **Pitch 6:** Send the face up and right, passing nine bolts (5.9, 130 feet). **Pitch 7:** Follow the S-shaped crack up through a small roof and to a bolted anchor (5.9, 165 feet). **Pitch 8:** Send the face, passing six bolts, to a ledge. This ledge has the unusual name of "The Snoring Prosthadonist Ledge" (5.9+, 130 feet). **Pitch 9:** Climb up through a roof, passing six bolts on the way (5.9+, 50 feet). **Pitch 10:** Continue up the amazing and steep pitch, passing twelve bolts before reaching an anchor (5.9, 110 feet). **Pitch 11:** Send the face, passing six bolts to attain a double-bolt anchor (5.9,

60 feet). **Pitch 12:** Climb straight up, passing four bolts. Trend left, working through some loose rock and clipping three more bolts. Climb up through a final bulge to the anchor (5.10c, 70 feet). **Descent:** Either rappel the route with double ropes, or join the Resolution Arête at pitch 14. Pro to 3 inches, 4 inches if continuing up the Resolution Arête. **FA:** Jorge Uriosite and Mike Clifford, 1997.

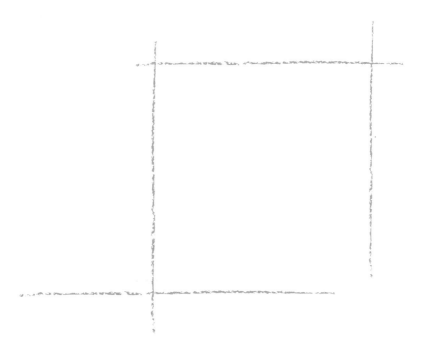

First Creek Canyon

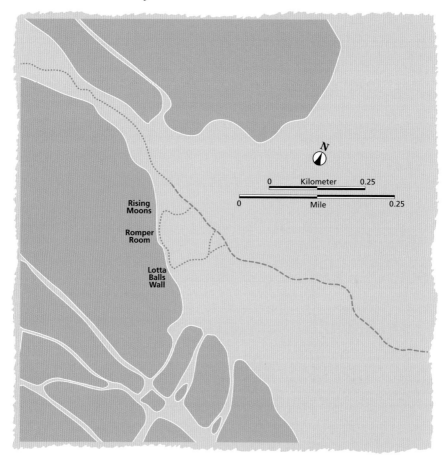

12.

First Creek Canyon

First Creek Canyon is found to the south of Mount Wilson. This cool area has some stellar multi-pitch climbing without the driving that's required for areas on the Red Rock Canyon Scenic Drive.

First Creek Canyon sits directly opposite a now-decommissioned gypsum mine. The old mine has been wildly controversial over the last few years, as developers fought to build subdivisions there, directly across the street from Red Rock Canyon.

Long ago, while the mine was still open, I was guiding Lotta Balls with a single climber. As I moved through the crux, the miners across the street detonated explosives. Startled, my student spun around on his stance and pulled wildly on the rope, ripping

First Creek Canyon Overview

me off my stance, causing an unexpected leader fall!

"What the . . ." I sputtered. "Why did you pull me off?!"

"I thought we were being attacked by Al-Qaeda!" he responded.

Rest assured that Al-Qaeda doesn't know about Red Rock Canyon. We know this for a fact. Because if they knew about climbing, they'd probably be much happier people and maybe we'd have a more peaceful world.

Approach: Drive 4.4 miles beyond the entrance to the Red Rock Canyon Scenic Drive. First Creek Canyon is on the right-hand side of the road and has a small sandy parking lot. Please be sure to park with your car's nose to the fence so that other vehicles may park in the same area. Take the very flat and sandy trail out of the parking lot and walk toward the "black square" of rock in the distance. There is some trail braiding. Eventually the trail will provide two options. Turn left and start working up the hill toward the Lotta Balls Wall if that is your destination, or drop down into the creek bed for a short period of time to reach the Romper Room Wall.

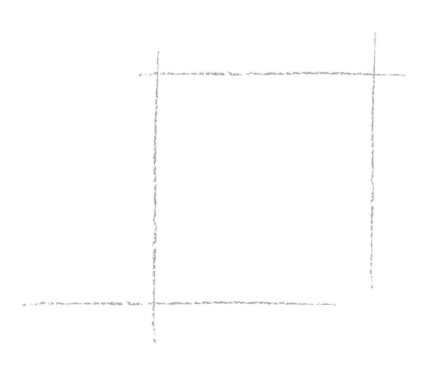

LOTTA BALLS WALL

Rest assured, this area is not named for the amount of courage needed to climb there. Instead, it is named after the fabulous Lotta Balls route, a crazy-cool 5.8 on the left-hand side of the wall that requires you to climb little marbles that feel like they're glued to the face.

Approach: From where the trail drops down into the creek, continue on the trail above the drainage. Eventually the trail starts to work steeply up the hillside to the base of Lotta Balls. **Time:** 1 hour.

Sun Exposure: This wall gets early morning sun, but is in the shade before 11 a.m. for most of the year. **Descent:** The descent for each of the following three routes is the same. Climb to the top of the feature and descend the gully that drops down to the right. Three single-rope rappels and some down-scrambling will bring you back and around to the base of the wall.

Types of Climbing Available: Moderate multi-pitch routes with some face and crack climbing

1. Lotta Balls (5.8+, II, 490 feet, trad) A way fun route. Start just right of the pillar leaning against the wall. **Pitch 1:** Climb up through a series of horizontals on the leaning boulder. From the top, continue up the left-facing corner and up a flake. Belay at a double-bolt anchor on a stance (5.6, 100 feet). **Pitch 2:** Climb up the marbles for 25 feet, clipping two bolts. Continue up the corner as the climbing grade eases, to a ledge and a bolted anchor (5.8+, 165 feet). Many people carry double ropes to this point and rappel. **Pitch 3:** Continue up the corner for 75 feet to a roof. Step left and follow the crack to a stance. Build a belay with trad gear (5.6, 175 feet). **Pitch 4:** Continue up easy terrain to the top of the feature (5.0, 50 feet). **Descent:** See descent info in this section's introduction. Pro to 4 inches. **FA:** Randal Grandstaff, Tom Kaufman, and Joe and Betsy Herbst, 1977.

2. Bruja's Brew (5.9, II, 490 feet, trad) This route is the line just to the right of Lotta Balls with a visible bolt. Start on top of the white boulder. **Pitch 1:** Climb up to the roof and break right. Clip a bolt and then continue up to the varnished wall beyond the corner. Clip a second bolt. Do not belay at the Lotta Balls anchor. Instead, continue up to the double-bolt belay on a ledge just a short distance farther (5.9, 130 feet). **Pitch 2:** Climb straight up the fantastic varnished face, angling slightly left. Build an anchor at a flaring crack below the roof (5.6, 140 feet). **Pitch 3:** Work up toward the right side of the roof on a ramp and then climb back left, following the line of weakness through the roof. Build an anchor at the alcove with a bush (5.7, 120 feet). Variation: Instead of going to the ramp and the line of weakness, find the crack to the left of

the ramp and climb directly through the roof, clipping a bolt along the way. Belay as for the pitch 3 description (5.8, 120 feet). **Pitch 4:** Continue up the easy crack to the top of the feature (5.5, 100 feet). **Descent:** See descent info in this section's introduction. Pro to 3 inches. **FA:** Todd Swain and Debbie Brenchley, 1991.

3. Black Magic (5.8, II, 490 feet, trad) This line works up the right-hand side of the feature. Start at a left-facing corner, 20 feet right of Bruja's Brew and 40 feet right of Lotta Balls. **Pitch 1:** Step up onto the boulder and climb the right-facing flake to the top. Clip a bolt and then continue up toward a second bolt. From there, continue up the corner and face, passing a third bolt to a belay at a natural thread. Place a piece or two in the crack to back this up for the belay (5.8, 140 feet). **Pitch 2:** Blast straight up easier, but more runout, varnished terrain to a double-bolt anchor (5.6, 150 feet). **Pitch 3:** Climb up and right, sending the short left-facing corner until you can step out right onto the arête. Clip a bolt and then step back left to get into another crack. Build a belay at a small ledge with bushes (5.6, 150 feet). **Pitch 4:** Climb up the easy crack to the top (5.4, 100 feet). **Descent:** See descent info in this section's introduction. Pro to 3 inches. **FA:** Jorge and Joanne Urioste, 1978.

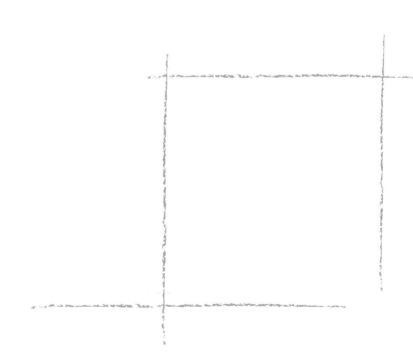

ROMPER ROOM

The Romper Room area, along with Moderate Mecca and the Ragged Edges Area, is a great place for beginning traditional leaders to practice their craft.

Approach: After dropping down into the creek bed from the main trail, continue weaving in and out of the creek bed until the "black square" is above the trail and drainage. A somewhat obvious rib cuts up from the drainage beyond this. Take the trail up the rib to the base of an easy chimney. This is the bottom of Rising Moons. The Romper Room routes are to the left of this and start on the left-hand side of the "black square." **Time:** 1 hour.

Sun Exposure: The area sees sun in the early morning, but goes into the shade well before noon.

Types of Climbing Available: Easy to moderate trad crack climbing; easy to moderate multi-pitch climbing

1. Guise and Gals (5.4, 80 feet, trad) The left-most route in the Romper Room area starts in a crack system directly behind a giant boulder. Climb up the low-angle, smooth, and

Romper Room

The left side of Romper Room

shallow dihedral to the anchors. Pro to 3 inches. **FA:** Kimi Harrison and Lesie Appling, 1992.

2. Girls and Buoys (5.5, 80 feet, trad) Found 20 feet right of Guise and Gals on the opposite side of the large boulder, this line climbs the left-most corner of a corner system that is composed of three corners. Send the corner for approximately 40 feet, then traverse left for a few feet until another corner appears. Continue up this to a double-bolt anchor. Pro to 3 inches. **FA:** Kimi Harrison and Leslie Appling, 1992.

3. Kindergarten Cop (5.7+, 140 feet, mixed) Found 25 feet right of Girls and Buoys under a triangular shaped roof. Climb a thin crack that pulls through the right-hand side of the roof and then clip the first of four pro-tection bolts. Continue up the middle of the white face to a double-bolt anchor. Make a double-rope rappel back to the ground. Pro to 4 inches, heavy on small gear. **FA:** Todd and Donette Swain, 1994.

4. Magic Mirror (5.5, 140 feet, trad) Found a few feet right of Kin-dergarten Cop, this line ascends a large left-facing corner and shares an anchor with that route. Make a double-rope rappel back to the ground. Pro to 3.5 inches. **FA:** Todd and Donette Swain, 1994.

5. Buzz Buzz (5.4, 75 feet, trad) This line is found 50 feet right of Magic Mirror and 20 feet left of the black varnished square. Climb a short low-angle dihedral to a double-bolt anchor. Pro to 3 inches. **FA:** Leslie Appling and Kimi Harrison, 1992.

6. Doobie Dance (5.6, 90 feet, trad) Climb the left-hand crack system on the varnished square. Pro to 3 inches. **FA:** Unknown.

7. Romper Room (5.7, 90 feet, trad) Send the intermittent crack system found just right of Doobie Dance in the center of the black varnished square. Pro to 4 inches. **FA:** Unknown.

Two very long single-rope rappels (tie knots!) down the gully from trees, and one short rappel

8. Algae on Parade (5.7+, II+, 580 feet, trad) A little-known classic line. Beware: There has been a beehive at the base of this route for several seasons. **Pitch 1:** Climb the right-hand side of the black varnished square up the left-facing corner. Climb up left of a bush. There is a bolt and some tat at the bush, but don't stop there. Climb left of the bush, then move right and build a belay on a roomy ledge (5.7+, 100 feet). **Pitch 2:** Climb straight up above the ledge toward the small tree/bush. Clip a bolt to the right of the tree. Follow the crack after the tree for 50 feet. Step right into a wider crack at a second bolt and build a belay (5.6, 100 feet). Variation: There are several ways to climb up to the bush. A slightly more fun way, but less well protected, is to climb up the varnished face to the same belay station. **Pitch 3:** Follow the crack system for nearly a full rope length. Build a belay on a tan ledge (5.6, 190 feet). **Pitch 4:** Continue up and right on easier terrain. Build a belay once at the top of the feature. Beware of loose blocks near the end of the pitch (5.2, 190 feet). **Descent:** Scramble down into the gully to climber's right—the gully between this route and Rising Moons—to a tree with slings. Make three rappels from trees. Rappel 1 is 100 feet, rappel 2 is 90 feet, and rappel 3 is 20 feet. After the rappels, some downclimbing and bushwhacking will take you back to the base of the wall. Pro to 4 inches. **FA:** John Martinet and Jeff Gordon, 1978.

9. Rising Moons (5.5, II-, 310 feet, trad) The first two pitches of this route provide an excellent experience for a beginning multi-pitch leader. The third pitch, while easy, requires big gear to sew it up, though many climbers do the top pitch with nothing bigger than a 4-inch piece. This line starts at the easy chimney at the top of the approach rib/hill. **Pitch 1:** Ascend the chimney. Build an anchor at the first flat area after exiting the chimney (5.2, 80 feet). Once your partner is up, battle a little bit of brush to move the anchor up to the base of a right-facing corner/chimney. **Pitch 2:** Climb the right-facing corner to a bolted belay (5.5, 140 feet). **Pitch 3:** Ascend the wide crack to the single bolt equalized to some bushes and build a belay. **Descent:** It's possible to descend the route with double ropes. It's also possible to scramble up and climber's left to the Algae on Parade descent gully (see descent info in the Algae on Parade route description). Pro to 4 or 5 inches. **FA:** Jono McKinny, 1990.

Black Velvet Canyon

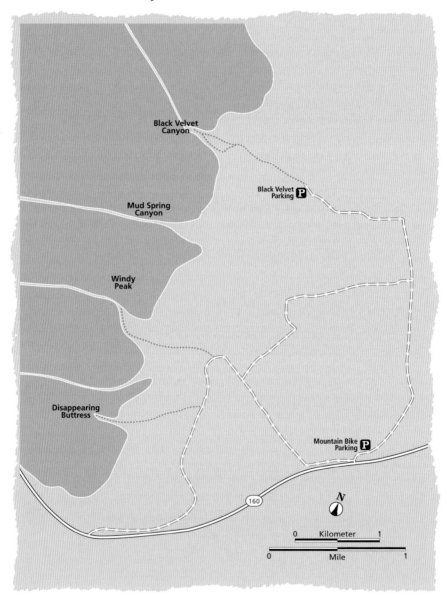

Black Velvet
Canyon

Mud Spring
Canyon

Windy
Peak

Disappearing
Buttress

Black Velvet
Parking

Mountain Bike
Parking

160

N

0   Kilometer   1

0   Mile   1

13.

Black Velvet Canyon

Black Velvet Canyon is a beautiful place. It is also home to several of the most well-known climbs in Red Rock. Names like Epinephrine, Dream of Wild Turkeys, and Frogland are known throughout the country by both those who have climbed in Red Rock and those who haven't.

The routes here vary in size and commitment. Some are large endeavors, whereas others are a bit more laid-back. There's something for everyone in this awe-inspiring canyon!

Approach: Black Velvet Canyon is outside the Red Rock Canyon Scenic Drive. From the entrance to the scenic drive, continue driving on NV 159 for about 10 miles to the junction with NV 160. Turn right (west) and drive 4.7 miles to a paved parking lot on the right. Turn off the highway and pass through the parking lot to a rough road on the right. Follow this road and pray that your car has high enough clearance. Most climbers are able to get rental cars down this road. At approximately 1.5 miles a spur road cuts away to the left. Do not turn. Continue on the main road for another 1.2 miles, veering left at the well-worn corner and eventually arriving at a small parking lot and the trailhead.

It may be tempting to camp in this lot. Many people get away with it. But some certainly don't. Occasionally the BLM raids this lot late at night and gives tickets to illegal campers. Don't say I didn't warn you!

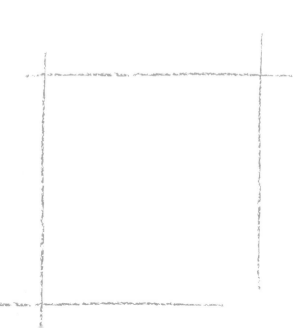

WHISKEY PEAK

Two peaks dominate the south walls of Black Velvet. The first and lower peak is Whiskey Peak. The second, taller peak is Black Velvet Peak.

Whiskey Peak is slightly more east than Velvet Peak. The first routes listed here are on this shorter of the two summits.

Approach: Hike the main trail into the canyon for approximately 20 minutes. Just before the trail drops into the wash, a well-traveled path cuts steeply up the hillside to the left. Take the left-hand trail and work up to the base of the cliffband. Scramble through the band and then follow braided trails to the base of the desired route. **Time:** 50 minutes.

If you are headed to the routes on the right (Triassic Sands, Wholesome Fullback, etc.), it's possible to approach them by traversing right past the Frogland area, but it's a bit easier to stay low and then cut up to the routes when you are closer.

Sun Exposure: These routes see early morning sun, but then fade into the shade.

Types of Climbing Available: Moderate to difficult multi-pitch climbing, crack and face climbing

1. Bourbon Street (5.8+, III, 800 feet, trad) This is a really good route with a similar character to Frogland. If you arrive at the base of Frogland and it's busy, this line provides an excellent backup plan. On the approach, look for the large white triangular roof in the buttress above the trail. Bourbon Street climbs up a crack system slightly to the right of this feature. At the base of the wall, there is a little step-across right before you get to the Frogland area. This climb starts shortly after the step-across, about 25 feet left of the base of Frogland, at a beautiful finger crack in a corner.

Pitch 1: Climb up the finger crack and corner to a ledge with some bushes. Step past these and then continue up the same system to a big ledge with a tree on it. This is the top of the first pitch of Frogland (5.7, 150 feet).

Pitch 2: Step right into the corner and begin to climb the shared pitch with Frogland. As you work up the corner, one crack shoots off to the left (Frogland) at a lower angle, while another crack goes up and right. Follow the crack up and right until it ends after approximately 70 feet. Step right to attain the upper part of the crack and follow this to a belay on a brushy ledge (5.8+, 120 feet).

Pitch 3: Go straight up through some bushes, aiming for the prominent buttress above the face. Follow the path of least resistance with the most protection up to the base of a steep headwall. This is about 40 feet below the belay, and it looks like there's no pro. Launch up onto the wall, where there is some gear, but expect it to be a little runout. Continue up the chocolate-colored face to a stance below a prominent buttress and build

a belay (5.6, 185 feet). **Pitch 4:** Step up and right to the lip under the buttress. Continue up and then left to the top of the lip where a flake appears. Climb up the flake to the end. Work through a bulge to a right-facing corner and then climb up to a series of small ledges (5.7+, 70 feet). **Pitch 5:** The goal is to stay left from here on out. Step left and climb a short finger crack to a right-leaning ramp. Follow the ramp until you reach a large horn. From the horn climb the face to an arête. Step left and climb toward a weakness in the summit overhangs. Belay on a ledge below a corner (5.6, 150 feet). **Pitch 6:** Step up and left to the corner and then climb the face. Continue up the corner to a large ledge. This pitch is short due to potential rope drag (5.7, 35 feet). **Pitch 7:** Climb up the face to the right and follow this to the summit (5.5, 35 feet). **Descent:** From the top of the feature, work down climber's left following cairns. Soon the saddle between Whiskey Peak and Black Velvet Peak comes into view. Walk down to the saddle and follow cairns to the left. Continue down the gully to the bottom. Work around the bottom of the feature to regain the base of the route. Pro to 4 inches. **FA:** Larry DeAngelo and John Wilder, 2005.

2. Frogland (5.8, III, 800 feet, trad)
This is an awesome route. On the approach, look for the large white triangular roof in the buttress above the trail. Frogland climbs the crack system immediately right of this feature. Start at the small white pillar leaning against the wall. **Pitch 1:** Climb up the white flake to the main crack system. Clip a bolt and then continue up the crack. Climb up the face to the left of the chimney. Continue past a bolt to easier climbing. Build an anchor at the tree (5.8, 150 feet). Variation 1: Climb the first pitch of Bourbon Street to avoid this pitch (5.7, 150 feet). Variation 2: Climb Raindance, the bolted face between the start of Frogland and Bourbon Street (5.10a R, 150 feet). **Pitch 2:** Climb up the crack system to the right of the tree. A dozen feet up the pitch, one crack continues to work its way right, while another cuts up to the left. Take the crack that leads to the left. Continue up the crack system to a small ledge and hangerless bolts. It's possible to belay here, but most continue up the chimney above. Climb the chimney until it pinches down, then move left and make a few face moves to reach another ledge. Build a belay station (5.7+, 150 feet). **Pitch 3:** Climb up the crack through the bulge, passing a large bush. Continue to work up the crack system to a small tree. Pass the tree and continue up to an alcove. Build a belay here (5.7, 100 feet). **Pitch 4:** Climb up and left of the alcove/ledge, working toward the roof. Easy climbing leads to a bolt. A few more easy moves lead to the roof. Traverse left under the roof to an arête. Climb up this feature

Frogland

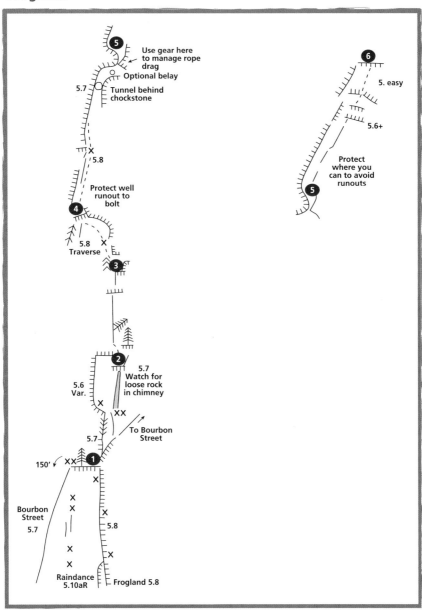

5 Use gear here to manage rope drag

Optional belay

5.7 Tunnel behind chockstone

X 5.8

Protect well runout to bolt

4

5.8 X
Traverse

3

2 5.7 Watch for loose rock in chimney

5.6 Var.

X

XX

5.7 To Bourbon Street

150' ↙ XX **1**

X

Bourbon Street 5.7

X
X

X
5.8

X

X

Raindance 5.10aR

Frogland 5.8

6 5. easy

5.6+

Protect where you can to avoid runouts

5

to a small stance and build an anchor (5.8, 75 feet). **Pitch 5:** Work up the crack system, passing a bolt. It's mildly runout just before the bolt. Step left and continue up the crack and corner to a giant chockstone. Tunnel underneath it and take care to sling your pro so it doesn't get pinched. Move right and climb around the corner to enter a small gully. Climb up the gully and build a belay at a nice ledge a few feet down and left of the top of the gully (5.8, 170 feet). **Note:** If you don't feel that you can keep your rope from getting pinched either behind the chockstone or at the turn around the corner above the chockstone, consider breaking the pitch into two, belaying on the ledge just above the chockstone. **Pitch 6:** Climb up the center of a slab with a few cracks for pro. This is a bit runout. Pull through a small bulge (crux) and continue up easier terrain to the top of the feature (5.6+, 150 feet). **Descent:** See the descent for Bourbon Street. Pro to 4 inches. **FA:** Jorge and Joanne Urioste, 1978.

3. Sand Felipe (5.10a, 120 feet, sport) This is a really fun little face climb that is found significantly to the right of Frogland. Follow the base of the wall until you come to a nicely bolted line. There are over twenty bolts on this route, and it feels very casual. The line can be broken into two short pitches if you don't have two ropes to rappel. **FA:** Unknown.

4. Triassic Sands (5.10b, III, 750 feet, trad) This was one of the first real climbs in Red Rock and is still considered to be one of the best 5.10 cracks in the conservation area. Found right of Sand Felipe are two corner systems. The corner system closer to Sand Felipe is the old aid start for Triassic Sands. Instead of starting there, go right to a left-facing corner. **Pitch 1:** Climb up the short left-facing corner to a big ledge (5.7, 40 feet). **Pitch 2:** Step out around the corner to the left and climb through a steep section using a combination of finger and hand jams. Follow the crack up as the difficulty eases and belay at a bolted anchor (5.10b, 120 feet). It is possible to combine the first two pitches. **Pitch 3:** Climb up the crack system to another fixed anchor (5.8, 150 feet). Many people rappel with double ropes from here. However, there is good climbing above. **Pitch 4:** Climb up the right-facing corner. Clip a bolt and be careful not to step on the flexing diving board feature. Continue up to a fixed anchor (5.10a, 160 feet). **Pitches 5 and 6:** Climb up easy 4th- and low 5th-class terrain to the top of the feature (5.0, 250 feet). **Descent:** Either rappel the route with double ropes before you run out of fixed anchors, or descend as per Bourbon Street. Pro to 3 inches with triples of 2- to 3-inch pieces. **FA:** Joe Herbst and Larry Hamilton, 1972. **FFA:** Augie Klein, Tom Kaufman, Randal Grandstaff, Chris Robbins, and Joe Herbst, 1979.

Triassic Sands
PHOTO BY ANDY STEPHEN

Whiskey Peak

Wholesome Fullback and Our Father
PHOTO BY DOUG FOUST

Optional belay

5

6

5. Wholesome Fullback (5.10b, II, 220 feet, trad) This wickedly cool line climbs the left side of a giant pillar lying against a buttress. The start of the route is found approximately 200 feet to the right of Triassic Sands. The base of the route is 10 feet right of a right-facing corner system, right of a pine tree on blocks. The first pitch climbs an obvious finger crack in varnished rock. **Pitch 1:** Climb up the thin crack, passing a crux near the bottom. Continue up to a nice hand crack and follow this up to a roof. Instead of climbing through the roof, traverse right to another crack. Make a few crux moves on this thin crack and then climb up another nice hand crack to a belay below a chimney (5.10b, 160 feet). It's also possible to stop and belay on a ledge approximately 50 feet up on the left. **Pitch 2:** Climb the chimney to the top of the pillar (5.7, 60 feet). **Note:** Many people elect to toprope the top of Our Father after finishing Wholesome Fullback. **Descent:** Rappel the route with double ropes, or rappel Our Father with a single rope. Pro to 3.5 inches with triples of 1- to 3-inch pieces. **FA:** Carl Folsom and Lars Holbeck, 1975.

6. Our Father (5.10d R, II, 240 feet, trad) This line climbs the other side of the pillar and feels stout! Find the base of this route approximately 25 feet to the right of Wholesome Fullback. The route starts in a right-leaning, left-facing corner. **Pitch 1:** Climb up the corner to a ledge with a tree (5.7+, 60 feet). **Pitch 2:** Climb up the runout slab above, passing two bolts. Arc left into the right-facing corner and make a few moves up onto a ledge. Belay at the double-bolt anchor (5.9, 100 feet). **Pitch 3:** Continue up the awesome corner to a bolted anchor (5.10d, 80 feet). **Descent:** Make three single-rope rappels. Pro to 3 inches. **FA:** Joe Herbst, Randal Grandstaff, Vern Clevenger, and Rich Wheeler, 1975.

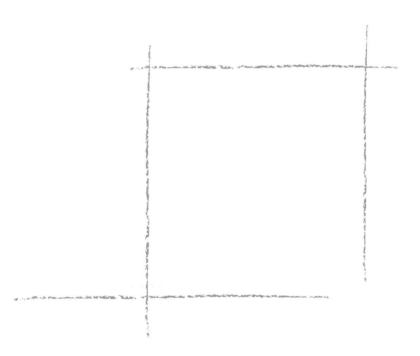

Black Velvet Peak

Black Velvet Wall
PHOTO BY MIKE LAYTON

BLACK VELVET PEAK

Black Velvet Peak is situated up and behind Whiskey Peak. There are two major features that people think of when they think of this peak. First, there's the Black Velvet Wall, a beautiful piece of steep rock that rises a thousand feet above the valley floor before there are any real breaks; and second, the Black Tower to the right of the wall. The Black Tower is well known for its association with Epinephrine, the famous route that climbs up the tower's right-hand side.

Be wary of people on the wall way up above you. Loose rocks are an obvious danger, but so too are dropped carabiners or water bottles. These things can do some real damage. Wear your helmet!

Approach: Follow the trail west out of the parking lot. Eventually you will come to a fork in the trail. One fork climbs the hill to Whiskey Peak, while the other continues straight and drops into the wash. Take the trail that continues straight. Drop into the wash and continue upstream. Eventually the creek bed is blocked by a small cliffband. Climb up left and out of the wash. Follow a steep trail up to the base of the Black Velvet Wall. If you are going to Epinephrine, climb around the band and then step back into the creek bed. Follow it up to the base of the route. **Time:** 50 minutes.

Sun Exposure: The Black Velvet Wall gets morning sun, but fades into the shade by 11 a.m. for most of the year.

Types of Climbing Available: Trad face and crack climbing, big multi-pitch lines

1. Refried Brains (5.9, III–IV, 600–2,000 feet, trad) This route has some really good climbing down low, but then the quality deteriorates. Only the first four pitches are recommended. This line is found on the left-hand side of the Black Velvet Wall, approximately 40 feet left of a massive block leaning against the wall at a crack that angles up right. **Pitch 1:** Climb up the crack and clip a bolt. Step up to a left-facing corner and pass another bolt. Scamper up to the anchor on the left (5.8+, 150 feet). **Pitch 2:** Climb up left into the corner system. Continue up this to the top of a pillar with a tree on it (5.8+, 150 feet). **Pitch 3:** Traverse right to reach a crack. Work up the crack toward the anchor. For the most part the crack is between 1 and 3 inches wide, but occasionally it's wider. Climb up and belay next to a tree (5.9, 150 feet). **Pitch 4:** Climb

up left through lower-angled terrain and some loose blocks to the base of a right-facing corner system. Note that there is an anchor here. Bypass the anchor and continue up the face (not the corner), passing four bolts. Step up to a double-bolt belay (5.9, 170 feet). **Note:** Many parties elect to descend from here with double-rope rappels. The upper pitches are notoriously loose. But if you want to go there . . . **Pitch 5:** Continue up the crack system to a less-than-inspiring fixed anchor (5.8, 150 feet). **Pitch 6:** Climb up a corner, passing a bolt to a ledge with a bolted anchor (5.7, 75 feet). **Pitch 7:** Continue up a crack. Choose between placing gear in between loosely stacked blocks or clipping an ancient bolt on one of said blocks. Decide that you're not going to fall. Finish on a ledge with an anchor (5.8, 130 feet). **Pitch 8:** Climb the corner to a treed ledge (5.7, 80 feet). **Pitches 9–14:** Continue up and right, above the Black Velvet Wall. Be extremely careful not to drop anything on climbers below, as this area is very loose. Follow your nose toward the summit on mostly 4th-class terrain with a little low 5th class thrown in for fun (5.4, 1,200 feet). **Descent:** See the descent for Epinephrine. Pro to 4 inches. **FA:** Stephanie Petrilak and Jorge and Joanne Urioste, 1979.

Black Velvet Peak

Black Velvet Wall
PHOTO BY ANDY STEPHEN

2. Prince of Darkness (5.10c, III, 650 feet, mixed) This route is both loved and hated. Those who like to move fast without a lot of gear love it. Those who want to climb the steepest and blankest part of the wall love it. Those who felt there were too many bolts on the route originally hated it. Today there are still those who dislike this route, but more because the movement is somewhat repetitive and all the belays are hanging than for the number of bolts. You know what I say to that? Just shut up and eat your awesome! You'll thank me for it. The route shares the first pitch with Dream of Wild Turkeys, and the base is found about 60 feet left of

Dream of Wild Turkeys

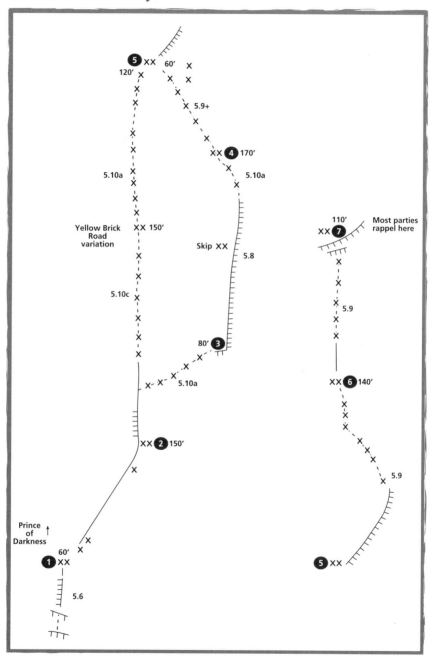

the giant arch that defines the right side of the wall. **Pitch 1:** Climb up the face to a crack. Continue up to a bolted anchor (5.6, 60 feet). **Pitch 2:** Follow a line of fourteen bolts up to another bolted anchor (5.10b, 110 feet). **Pitch 3:** Climb up to a crack and place a few traditional pieces before climbing past more bolts (fifteen all together) to another bolted anchor (5.10a, 130 feet). **Pitch 4:** Follow the line of fourteen bolts to a bolted anchor (5.9, 130 feet). **Pitch 5:** Climb up and left, following a crack. Continue past eight bolts to an anchor (5.9, 120 feet). **Pitch 6:** Climb up into the crux of the climb. Cross the slab, following a shallow crack. The climbing eases as you move up to a much-needed ledge and the final anchor. There are thirteen bolts on this pitch, and the final belay anchor is shared with Dream of Wild Turkeys (5.10c, 100 feet). **Descent:** Rappel the route with double ropes. Pro to 2 inches. **FA:** Jorge and Joanne Urioste, 1980.

3. Dream of Wild Turkeys (5.10a, IV–IV+, 1,000–2,000 feet, mixed) At the time of its first ascent, this was a visionary line. Thin cracks and corners are linked together by a handful of bolts on a line that is mostly 5.9. The exposure, the position, and the movement on this line are—to put it bluntly—awesome! The first pitch is shared with Prince of Darkness. **Pitch 1:** Climb up the face to a crack. Continue up to a bolted anchor (5.6, 60 feet). **Pitch 2:** Step up and right,

passing two bolts, to gain a right-leaning crack. Follow the crack up to a double-bolt anchor on a small ledge (5.9, 150 feet). **Pitch 3:** Continue up the crack until a line of bolts appears on the face to the right. Traverse past five bolts to a ledge and an anchor (5.10a, 80 feet). Variation: Instead of going right, continue straight up for two pitches following the bolt line. This is the Yellow Brick Road variation, and the pitches are 5.10c and 5.10a. The variation rejoins Dream of Wild Turkeys at the top of pitch 5. **Pitch 4:** Follow the crack up to the top. It starts wide at the bottom and then constricts until it disappears. Pass two bolts on the slab above the crack (crux) and then climb up to the bolted belay station (5.10a, 170 feet). **Pitch 5:** Arc up and left across the slab, passing five bolts to another bolted anchor at the bottom of a corner (5.9+, 60 feet). **Pitch 6:** Climb up and right into the crescent-shaped corner. Continue up this to another bolted line. Follow seven bolts across the face as they arc back to a bolted belay station (5.9, 140 feet). **Pitch 7:** Continue up a thin crack. Once that peters out, climb up the face, passing five bolts to an anchor at a scoop (5.9, 110 feet). **Note:** Most parties rappel with double ropes from here. If you choose to do that, rappel straight down over the Yellow Brick Road variation. **Pitch 8:** Zig up and right and then zag back left to a bolt anchor at the bottom of a steep wall (5.0, 80 feet). **Pitch 9:** Climb up thin cracks, passing seven

Sour Mash

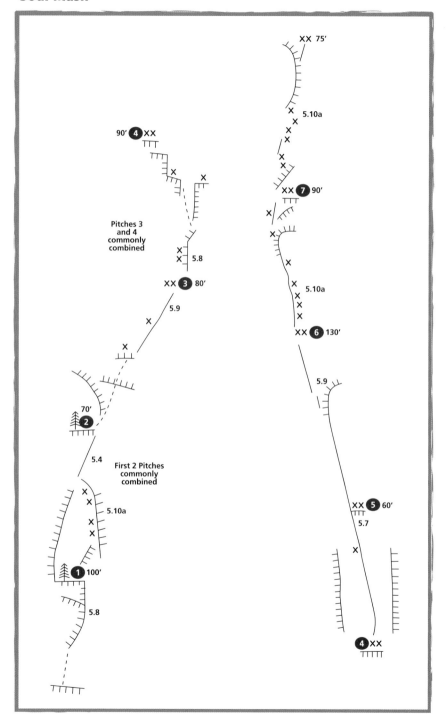

bolts to a bolted anchor (5.9, 140 feet). **Pitch 10:** Step left and climb up, passing four bolts to a crack. Continue up to a bolted anchor at the top (5.9, 150 feet). **Note:** This is the last chance to rappel without surrendering gear. If you climb beyond here, you're going to the top. **Pitch 11:** Work up the face and crack, passing one bolt to a large ledge known as the "Turkeyland Ledge" (5.7, 160 feet). **Upper Pitches:** This line joins Refried Brains and climbs up 3rd-, 4th- and low 5th-class terrain to reach the summit. Much of this terrain is loose and not recommended. The final 1,000 feet requires four to five pitches (5.4, 1,000 feet). **Descent:** If you climb to the top, descend via the Epinephrine descent. Otherwise, rappel with double ropes straight down the face. Follow the Yellow Brick Road variation for a more direct descent. Pro to 4 inches. **FA:** Jorge and Joanne Urioste, 1980.

4. Sour Mash (5.10a, III, 700 feet, trad) This line is very similar to Dream of Wild Turkeys in both its level of difficulty as well as its fun factor. It's not uncommon for Prince of Darkness and Dream of Wild Turkeys to have several parties on them, while Sour Mash sits empty. Toward the right-hand side of the Black Velvet Wall is a giant arcing roof. Sour Mash climbs up the main crack system to the right of this feature. Start on the right side of the giant roof, left of a triangular buttress. **Pitch 1:** Climb up the face to the right-facing crack

to a ledge with a tree (5.8, 100 feet). **Pitch 2:** Continue up the right-hand side of the triangular feature (5.10a). Clip four bolts before exiting the feature and attaining easier 5.4 ground. Scramble up to a belay next to a tree (5.10a, 70 feet). **Note:** Pitch 1 and pitch 2 are commonly linked. **Pitch 3:** Climb up and right, then continue straight up through a bulge and clip two bolts. After the second bolt, continue to diagonal up and right, following a crack to an anchor (5.9, 80 feet). **Pitch 4:** Climb straight up the thin crack above, then pass two bolts on the face. Arc back left over a ledge and clip another bolt. Continue from there up left to an anchor (5.8, 90 feet). **Note:** Pitches 3 and 4 may be linked. **Pitch 5:** There are three crack systems above this anchor. Take the central crack up to a hanging belay at a bolted anchor (5.7, 60 feet). **Pitch 6:** Continue up the mildly left-leaning crack. Eventually you will have to step out of it to the left. Make a couple of face moves before attaining another crack. This will take you to a bolted belay (5.9, 130 feet). **Pitch 7:** Continue up the thin crack, passing six bolts. Lieback through a few moves and then step left to clip two more bolts before reaching the bolted anchor on the right end of a white roof (5.10a, 90 feet). **Pitch 8:** Climb up and left, moving through the white roof and passing two bolts. Continue up a thin crack until you reach a face. Climb up right, passing three bolts and then cut back left, passing another bolt to

Rachel Spitzer inches up a chimney pitch on Epinephrine.
Photo by Jonathon Spitzer

reach a left-facing corner. Work up the corner, passing one more bolt, to reach an anchor (5.10a, 75 feet). **Descent:** Rappel the route with double ropes. It's also possible to rappel just left of the route. This secondary rappel line requires four double-rope rappels and one single-rope rappel to reach the ground. Pro to 3 inches. **FA:** Jorge and Joanne Urioste, 1980.

5. Epinephrine (5.9, IV+, 2,200 feet, trad) This is arguably the most famous route in Red Rock. The line is beautiful and the position is beyond compare.

The one thing everybody thinks they know about this line is that it is chimney heavy. This isn't quite true. The route can be broken into three major sections. The first section is the chimney section, the second is the face section, and the third and final is the mid-5th-class section. Each of these sections is approximately five pitches long.

The one thing that everybody should know about this route is that the grade is stiff for Red Rock. People who are leading 5.9 in the Black Corridor will have a hard time with the bottom of this route. It's not a bad idea for those who aren't sure of themselves to try something similar, but shorter, first. Community Pillar in Pine Creek Canyon is a good warm-up. If you can do that route reasonably fast, you'll be fine on Epinephrine. If you're not sure of yourself, bring a second rope to ensure that you don't have to leave gear if you're forced to bail.

Epinephrine climbs the right-hand side of the Black Tower. From there the line goes straight up the face until it reaches a ramp that leads off to the right. The line climbs right to the summit of Black Velvet Peak. Start at the base of the Black Tower on the right-hand side. A line of four bolts goes straight up a gray slab.

Pitch 1: Follow the line of bolts up out of the wash to a bushy ledge (5.8). Continue up a short left-facing corner to another bolt. Move across the 5.7 slab to a bolt. Climb straight up to another corner and follow this to a bolted belay station (5.8, 160 feet). **Pitch 2:** Climb up into your first chimney. Stay inside until it makes sense to step out right onto easier face climbing. Scamper up this to a belay at the base of the daunting chimney system above (5.8, 150 feet). **Pitch 3:** Climb up the main chimney and then step out to a ledge and an anchor on the right. This anchor can feel a bit hidden. Climb to it as the chimney widens. You'll note at this point that the insides of this chimney feel like glass (5.9, 110 feet). **Pitch 4:** Arguably the crux of the route. Continue up the chimney, moving through a flaring section. Bypass an anchor (or use it if you're worked) and continue to worm your way up. Just below the next belay station, look for a hand crack on the right. Climb this to the anchor (5.9, 150 feet). **Pitch 5:** Step off the anchor and back into the chimney. Clip two bolts and then continue up to the top of the Black Tower

Epinephrine

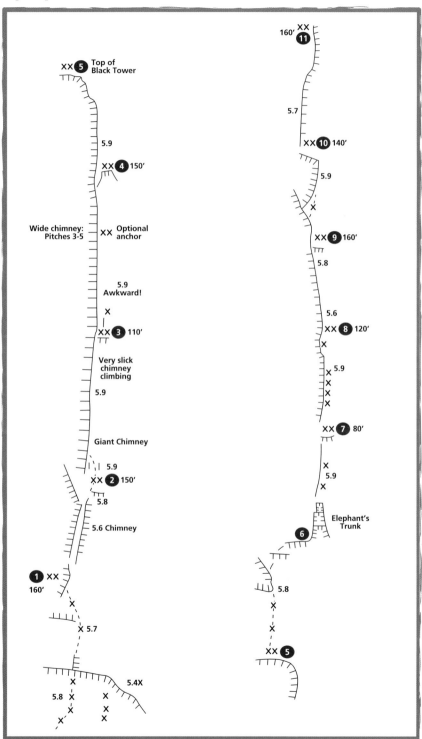

160' XX
11

5.7

XX 10 140'

5.9

X

XX 9 160'

5.8

5.6

XX 8 120'

X

5.9
X
X
X
X

XX 7 80'

X
5.9
X

Elephant's
Trunk

6

5.8
X

X

X

XX 5

XX 5 Top of
Black Tower

5.9

XX 4 150'

Wide chimney: XX Optional
Pitches 3-5   anchor

5.9
Awkward!

X

XX 3 110'

Very slick
chimney
climbing

5.9

Giant Chimney

5.9

XX 2 150'

5.8

5.6 Chimney

1 XX
160'

X

X 5.7

X   5.4X
5.8 X   X
X   X
X

Epinephrine

(5.9, 120 feet). **Pitch 6:** The climbing eases from here. The face climbing feels much more like it does in the Calico Hills. Climb straight up the face above, passing two bolts (5.6). Climb up through a bulge (5.8) and then work right, passing a little tree to the base of a series of stacked blocks. This is known as the "Elephant's Trunk" (5.8, 150 feet). **Pitch 7:** Climb up the Trunk and onto the face. Clip two bolts and then belay at a bolted anchor at a stance (5.9, 80 feet). **Pitch 8:** Climb up the left-facing corner, passing five bolts to a belay station (5.9, 120 feet). **Pitch 9:** Continue up the left-facing corner. The base of the corner is 5.6, but as you go up it gets a bit harder. The crux is a short section of 5.8 fingers. Belay at a bolted anchor (5.8, 160 feet). **Pitch 10:** Continue to climb the corner until it makes more sense to launch out onto the face. Clip a bolt and then return to the corner. Eventually you will reach a roof. Either climb 5.9 jugs on the left side of the roof, or delicately climb through fragile 5.8 flakes on the right side. Climb up through easier terrain to an alcove and a bolted belay (5.9, 140 feet). **Pitch 11:** Continue up the low-angle, left-facing corner to the base of a large right-leaning ramp (5.7, 160 feet). **Pitches 12-14:** Climb up the ramp to a tree on the left side of a ledge system (5.4, 500 feet). **Pitch 15:** Traverse right across the ledge to a giant tree (4th class, 200 feet). **Pitch 16:** Scramble to the summit (2nd class, 200 feet). Pro to 4 inches. Some may wish to have a 5-inch piece.

Doubles in the 4-inch range might be nice. Triples in the 1- to 3-inch range may be desirable if you're climbing near your limit. **FA:** Joe Herbst and Jorge and Joanne Urioste, 1978.

Descent: This descent is complex and can be very difficult in the dark. If you've had the opportunity to climb Bourbon Street or Frogland, you've done the bottom part of the descent. The saddle between Black Velvet Peak and Whiskey Peak is a major waypoint. Don't descend any gullies anywhere until you feel like you can reach this saddle. It's farther down the ridgeline than you might think.

If you're even considering a rappel, you've taken a wrong turn! Climb back up on the ridge and try again! If you can't see and you're repeatedly getting stymied, it might be better to wait until morning and walk out in the light.

From the top of Black Velvet Peak, scramble down southeast on the ridge. Do not go down the first gully you come to. Instead, continue to follow cairns along the ridge for approximately half a mile.

At the time of this writing, a giant cairn marked the descent down left (northeast) toward the saddle. Follow the climber's trail and cairns steeply down to the saddle between Black Velvet Peak and Whiskey Peak. From there, drop down the trail to the right (southeast), and continue down the well-traveled descent route to the base of Whiskey Peak toward the parking lot.

Vivian DeBros works through
the traverse on Jubilant Song.
PHOTO BY ZACH NOVAK

14.

Windy Peak

Approach: From the entrance to the Red Rock Canyon Scenic Drive, continue on NV 159. Pass the small town of Blue Diamond and the gypsum mine. After 10 miles, make a right-hand turn onto NV 160. From there you have two options: The first is to turn right on NV 160 and drive 4.7 miles to a small turnoff and paved parking lot on the right-hand side of the road. From the parking lot, follow the rough road on the right for 1.4 miles. Turn left and follow the slightly rougher spur road for an additional mile. Park at a small pullout that was formerly a jeep road.

The second option may be mildly shorter; however, it will be a lot harder on your vehicle. Take NV 160 to the same parking lot. Instead of pulling off the road, continue 0.25 mile farther on the highway and pull off shortly after a green sign. Follow very rough roads while working toward

Windy Peak

the first drainage north of the high-way. Park as close as possible without damaging your car. These two road options eventually meet one another. So ideally you can park at the same location regardless of the driving approach.

Hike the jeep road for approximately 5 minutes until it bisects a mountain-bike trail. Follow the trail for 15 to 20 minutes, working toward Windy Peak. Eventually the trail comes to a small watering tub for horseback riders and burros. Take braided trails from the tub around the mountain toward the south side. Eventually you will reach a steep rib to the left of a deep gully below the south face. Do not go up the gully. Instead, hike up the steep rib on a good trail to the base of the south face of Windy Peak. **Time:** 1.5 hours.

Sun Exposure: This face is in the sun all day. However, the peak isn't called Windy Peak for nothing. It's not a good place to visit in a windstorm.

Types of Climbing Available: Moderate, more well-established adventure climbing, crack and face climbing

1. Jubilant Song (5.8, IV, 900 feet, trad) This line follows a massive corner system up the south face of Windy Peak. The route starts on the left side of the face on the left-hand of two parallel cracks. **Pitch 1:** Climb up the left-hand crack, passing a small roof,

to a ledge with a bush (5.7, 100 feet). **Pitch 2:** Continue up the corner and into a wide chimney. Beware of loose blocks. Build a belay on top of the blocks (5.7, 150 feet). **Pitch 3:** Climb up and right, following the corner. Climb up an easy chimney. Continue past a large ledge to a smaller one, below a huge roof. Build a belay on the left-hand side of the roof at a stance below a small roof (5.5, 60 feet). **Pitch 4:** Climb up beneath the roof and traverse right to a small right-facing corner. Climb up the corner and belay at a stance (5.7, 60 feet). **Pitch 5:** Blast straight up through the small roof. Make a thin move in the corner and then move up to easier terrain. Build a belay next to a bush (5.8, 60 feet). Variation: It is possible to avoid the hardest moves on this pitch by moving out to the right and working up the face (5.5). **Pitch 6:** Climb up the gully above. Move into a chimney and then up to a bush. Step right and send the water groove, passing a bolt. Move up through some balancy terrain and then step left to a ledge (5.7, 100 feet). **Pitch 7:** Continue up the sparsely protected water groove. Step left from the groove and climb up the corner to a ledge. This pitch is a bit runout (5.8, 100 feet). Variation: From the top of pitch 6, climb up left on the face, then arc back right to attain the same ledge as the prior option (5.5, 100 feet). **Pitch 8:** Scramble up and left to attain the

Jubilant Song

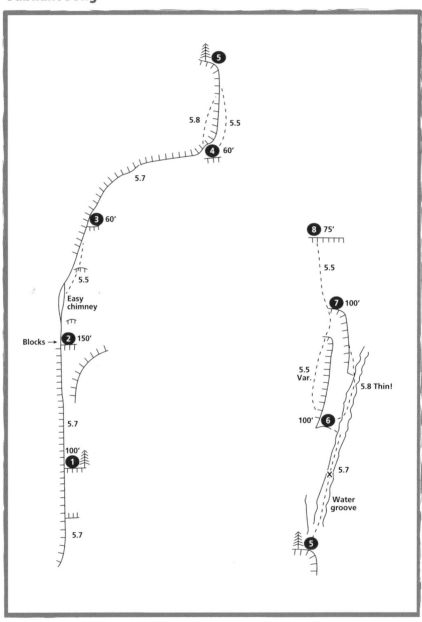

summit (5.5, 75 feet). **Descent:** Hike up to the top of Windy Peak and then go west toward the limestone at the top of Windy Canyon. When you reach a gully full of trees, cut left (south) and drop down. Follow cairns as you climb out of the gully and attain a small rib that goes east, toward the base of the wall. Follow the rib down to the bottom of the route. Pro to 4 inches. **FA:** Joe Herbst and Terry Schultz, 1972.

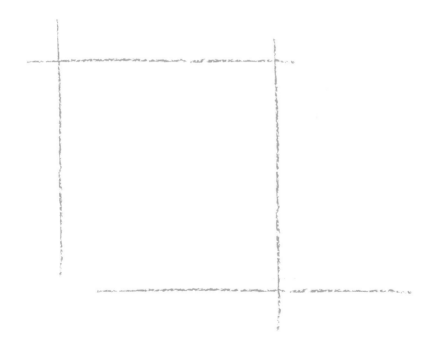

Disappearing Buttress

15.

Disappearing Buttress

It's truly amazing how often new features are discovered in Red Rock Canyon. The Disappearing Buttress was rediscovered in 2009. It's likely that it had been visited in the distant past, but there was no record. After the first route went in, several more followed in short order. At the time of this writing, there were nine established lines in the area, with a lot of room for more!

Approach: From the entrance to the Red Rock Canyon Scenic Drive, continue on NV 159. Pass the small town of Blue Diamond and the gypsum mine. After 10 miles, make a right-hand turn onto NV 160. From there you have two options: The first is to turn right on NV 160 and drive 4.7 miles to a small turnoff and paved parking lot on the right-hand side of the road. From the parking lot, follow the rough road on the right for 1.4 miles. Turn left and follow the slightly rougher spur road for an additional mile. Pass the pullout for Windy Peak and continue to the next pullout.

The second option may be mildly shorter; however, it will be a lot harder on your vehicle. Take NV 160 to the same parking lot. Instead of pulling off the road, continue 0.25 mile farther on the highway and pull off

shortly after a green sign. Follow very rough roads while working toward the first drainage north of the highway. Park as close as possible without damaging your car. These two road options eventually meet one another.

Take braided trails out of the parking lot toward the largest drainage north of the highway and south of Windy Peak. As you approach the mouth of the canyon, cross to the right side of the wash and follow mildly better trails into the canyon. The Disappearing Buttress is the 500-foot-tall buttress a short distance into the canyon. Prime Rib climbs the prominent line on the south face. Pricks and Ticks climbs a crack system just to the right of it. **Time:** 1 hour.

Sun Exposure: These routes get sun all day.

Types of Climbing Available: Moderate multi-pitch lines with no crowds, but a bit of crumbly rock. In other words, adventure climbs!

1. Prime Rib (5.7, II, 540 feet, trad) This line climbs up the crest of the buttress. It's a bit runout at times and has some loose rock, so it might not be the best choice for a budding 5.7 leader. But it is a really fun route! **Pitch 1:** From the toe of the south face, scramble up 4th-class terrain with an occasional 5th-class move to a large ledge, just below and left of a pine tree (5.0, 120 feet). **Pitch 2:** Climb up a crack system just to the right of the crest. Step up to the actual buttress and bypass a small square roof. Build a belay just above (5.7, 120 feet). **Pitch 3:** Continue up just right of the crest. Follow a curving crack up the face. Step up to the top of a pillar and build a belay (5.6, 100 feet). **Pitch 4:** Climb up steep varnished plates, gradually working up and right. Step up onto a large ledge and build a belay (5.7, 150 feet). **Pitch 5:** Climb up the gully above and right. Finish left of a large boulder (5.4, 50 feet). **Descent:** Walk west (up-canyon) and contour back down to the base. Pro to 3 inches. **FA:** Maurice Horn, Andrew Carson, Bill Hotz, and Jorge Urioste, 2009.

2. Pricks and Ticks (5.9, II, 500 feet, trad) This route is found just up and to the right of Prime Rib. It climbs up the obvious curving crack and then continues to the summit of the feature. The route was named "Pricks and Ticks" because one of the first ascensionists had the misfortune to fall into a cactus on the descent. In addition to that, it seemed like the team was battling an unusually large number of ticks throughout the day. **Pitch 1:** Climb the beautiful arching crack up to a ledge. Most of the crack is 5.7, but as it squeezes down and traverses, it becomes 5.9. Belay at an anchor (5.9, 160 feet). **Pitch 2:** Climb up past a brushy ledge and onto the arête. The black patina on the arête is similar to that found on Armatron in Juniper Canyon or Going Nuts in Oak Creek Canyon, but much less sustained. As the rock quality deteriorates, step left onto a ledge and build a belay (5.7, 100 feet). **Pitch 3:** Climb a chimney up and right. Continue to traverse right to a belay ledge at the base of a large corner (5.5, 75 feet). **Pitch 4:** Climb up the corner to the summit. More good black rock is found on this spectacular pitch. At the top, be sure to put in directionals so that the rope doesn't knock loose rock onto your partners (5.7, 160 feet). **Descent:** Descend as for Prime Rib. Walk west (up-canyon) and contour back down to the base. Pro to 4 inches. **FA:** Kevin Hogan, Dyan Padagas, and Jason Martin, 2010.

Appendix A—
Las Vegas Climber Resources

EMERGENCY

In the event of an emergency, call 911. Professional search and rescue police officers from the Las Vegas Metro Police Department will usually respond. In most cases they do so with a helicopter. Once a patient is packaged at an accident site, the helicopter transports the patient to the road where paramedics take over with an ambulance. Most injuries are treated at the University Medical Center.

Hospitals

University Medical Center

1800 W. Charleston Blvd.
Las Vegas, NV 89102
(702) 383-2000
This is a Level I trauma center and perhaps the best place to take a seriously injured patient. This is where those rescued by search and rescue tend to be taken.

From the entrance to the Red Rock Canyon Scenic Drive, drive east on Charleston Boulevard (NV 159) for 15 miles, or approximately 35 minutes. The hospital is on the left (north) side of the road, just west of I-215.

Summerlin Hospital Medical Center

657 N. Town Center Dr.
Las Vegas, NV 89144
(702) 233-7000
Summerlin Hospital has excellent emergency services and is just 15 minutes from the Red Rock Canyon Scenic Drive.

From the entrance to the Red Rock Canyon Scenic Drive, drive east on Charleston Boulevard (NV 159) for 6.2 miles. Turn left on Town Center Drive and drive 2 miles to the Summerlin Hospital.

SHOWERS

There's no such thing as a free lunch or a free shower. But you can find a shower relatively close to the conservation area:

Veterans Memorial Leisure Services Center

101 N. Pavilion Center Dr.
Las Vegas, NV 89144
(702) 229-1100

Red Rock Climbing Center

8201 W. Charleston Blvd.
Las Vegas, NV 89117
(702) 254-5604

GEAR AND EQUIPMENT
Desert Rock Sports
8221 W. Charleston Blvd.
Las Vegas, NV 89117
(702) 254-1143

REI—Summerlin
710 S. Rampart Blvd.
Las Vegas, NV 89145
(702) 951-4488

REI—Green Valley Ranch
220 Village Walk Dr., Suite 150
Henderson, NV 89052

CLIMBING GYMS
Red Rock Climbing Center
8201 W. Charleston Blvd., Suite 150
Las Vegas, NV 89117
(702) 254-5604
redrockclimbingcenter.com

Origin: Climbing and Fitness
7585 Commercial Way, Suite J
Henderson, NV 89011
(702) 570-7030
originclimb.com
American Alpine Institute guides may
be booked out of Origin.

Nevada Climbing Centers
3065 E. Patrick Ln., Suite 4
Las Vegas, NV 89120
(702) 898-8192
nvclimbing.com

The Refuge: Climbing and Fitness
6283 S. Valley View Blvd., Suite C
Las Vegas, NV 89118
climbrefuge.com

Appendix B—Climbing Instruction

Selecting an appropriate guide service is a complex decision. Perhaps the best way to determine if a given service is appropriate for you is to evaluate the company's professionalism. To do this, you must first pose a series of questions to the guide service.

- What are the company's training requirements?
- Has my guide completed any industry standard–type training such as that provided by the American Mountain Guides Association (AMGA) or the equivalent?
- Does the company employ AMGA trained/certified guides? And if so, will I have one?
- What are the company's medical training requirements?
- How long has my guide been guiding?
- How long has the company been in operation?
- Has the company had any accidents? And if so, why?
- If the trip will take place outside the guide's home base, how familiar is the guide with the destination?

Once you've completed this, you'll need to evaluate the guide service's answers carefully. Did it feel like they were being honest?

Additionally you should ask yourself the following questions about the company's professionalism after you complete your program.

- Did I receive the guide that I was promised?
- Did the guide/company represent the guide's level of training and certification appropriately?
- Did I feel safe with the guide?
- Did the guide act professionally throughout the program?
- Did the guide treat me with respect?
- Did the company or guide return e-mails and phone calls quickly?

Several guide services operate regularly in Red Rock Canyon National Conservation Area, including the American Alpine Institute, Jackson Hole Mountain Guides, Red Rock Climbing Center, Mountain Skills, and the National Outdoor Leadership School.

The author recommends the following guide service and the

following event to those looking for guided climbing or climbing instruction:

AMERICAN ALPINE INSTITUTE
(360) 671-1505
alpineinstitute.com
AAI is a world-class guide service that employs local AMGA trained and certified guides. AAI guides are deeply involved in Red Rock Canyon access and conservation efforts, while also continuing to establish new climbs throughout the conservation area.

RED ROCK RENDEZVOUS
Mountain Gear, a climbing equipment retailer, sponsors a three-day climbing festival in Red Rock Canyon National Conservation Area and at Spring Mountain Ranch State Park every spring. During the day, world-class climbing athletes and guides provide clinics on dozens of different climbing-related subjects for all skill levels. And at night, everybody gets together to eat, drink, dance, and play stupid climber games.

Red Rock Rendezvous provides an inexpensive alternative to professional instruction and guiding. And it's also incredibly fun!

Appendix C—Important Contacts, Websites, and Books

RED ROCK CANYON VISITOR INFORMATION

Red Rock Canyon Visitor Center
(702) 515-5350
Las Vegas BLM General Number
(702) 515-5000
Late Exit Permits
(702) 515-5050

PERTINENT ONLINE INFORMATION

Red Rock Canyon National Conservation Area
(www.blm.gov/nv/st/en/fo/lvfo/
blm_programs/blm_special_areas/
red_rock_nca.html)

Southern Nevada Climbers Coalition (www.lvclimbers council.org)
Formerly, the Las Vegas Climbers Liaison Council, this is a climber's advocacy group with a focus on Red Rock Canyon and other climbing areas in Southern Nevada.

Mountain Project Nevada (www .mountainproject.com)
Provides up-to-date information on routes both old and new throughout Red Rock Canyon.

Las Vegas Metro Police Department Search and Rescue (lvmpd sar.blogspot.com)

Red Rock Search and Rescue (redrocksar.org)

BOOK RESOURCES FOR CLIMBING IN RED ROCK CANYON

Red Rocks, A Climber's Guide II
By Jerry Handren

The Red Rocks of Southern Nevada
By Joanne Urioste

Red Rock Canyon, The Red Book Supplement
By Joanne Urioste

Red Rock Canyon: A Climbing Guide
By Roxanna Brock and Jared McMillen
Mountaineers Books

Red Rock Odyssey
By Larry DeAngelo and Bill Thiry
Verex Press

Red Rocks Climbing
By Greg Barns
Supertopo

Rock Climbing, Red Rocks
By Todd Swain
FalconGuides

Southern Nevada Bouldering II
By Tom Moulin
Snell Press

Fun Climbs Red Rocks: Topropes and Moderates
By Jason D. Martin
Sharp End Publishing

Index

About the Author

Jason D. Martin is an AMGA-certified Rock Guide, the director of operations for the American Alpine Institute, and a freelance writer. Much of Jason's adventure writing revolves around the work that he does in the mountains. Jason has logged innumerable days guiding in Red Rock Canyon, but also in the Cascades, the Sierra, Joshua Tree National Park, the Alaska Range, the Coast Mountains of Canada, and the Andes of Bolivia, Ecuador, and Peru. He authored *Fun Climbs Red Rocks: Topropes and Moderates* and coauthored *Washington Ice: A Climbing Guide*, and *Rock Climbing: The AMGA Single Pitch Manual.* Jason has put up dozens of first ascents in Red Rock Canyon, served on the board of directors for the Las Vegas Climbers Liaison Council for eight years, and serves as the technical director for the annual Red Rock Rendezvous climbing festival. In addition to writing about climbing and mountaineering, Jason is a playwright and film critic.

Follow Jason's outdoor, guiding, and writing adventures at:
   Instagram—AlpineInstitute
   Twitter—@AlpineInstitute
   Facebook—AlpineInstitute

Jason D. Martin
PHOTO BY JAY HACK